ETHICS
A BRIEF INTRODUCTION

ETHICS

A BRIEF INTRODUCTION

Robert C. Solomon
University of Texas at Austin

McGraw-Hill, Inc.

New York   St. Louis   San Francisco   Auckland   Bogotá   Caracas   Hamburg
Lisbon   London   Madrid   Mexico   Milan   Montreal   New Delhi   Paris
San Juan   São Paulo   Singapore   Sidney   Tokyo   Toronto

This book was set in Times Roman by University Graphics, Inc. (ECU).
The editors were Anne Murphy and David Dunham;
the production supervisor was Diane Renda.
The cover was designed by Joan E. O'Connor;
the cover collage was assembled by Mark Yankus.
R. R. Donnelley & Sons Company was printer and binder.

ETHICS

A Brief Introduction

    4 5 6 7 8 9 0   DOC/DOC   9 9 8 7 6 5 4 3 2 1

ISBN 0-07-059658-1

Library of Congress Cataloging in Publication Data

Solomon, Robert C.
    Ethics: a brief introduction.

    Includes index.
    1. Ethics. I. Title.
BJ1012.S568   1984   170   83-19596
ISBN 0-07-059658-1

For my brothers,
Andy and Jon

CONTENTS

PREFACE

In this book I have tried to provide a short introduction to ethics. Briefly defined, ethics is the study of the rules of right and wrong behavior, the appreciation and justification of the goals we strive for, and the ideals we admire, and the laws we think it right and necessary to obey. It is a general set of answers to the question, "What should I do?" Accordingly, the subject matter of ethics is as broad-ranging as human behavior itself, covering such daily matters as sexual conduct, family loyalties, and the rules against cheating on exams as well as the life-and-death issues of the morality of abortion and suicide, one's obligation to risk one's life in the armed services in times of war, and the right of a society to take the lives of its criminals.

The study of ethics is the attempt to clarify our thinking about the most general goals, ideals, rules, and principles which govern our conduct in all such matters. For example, all three of the life-and-death issues mentioned above involve one of our most fundamental ethical principles, which is sometimes summarized as the individual's "right to life." We enter into our study of ethics with the unshakable conviction that people should not be killed or forced to risk their lives, or at least, not without a very good reason. But what is a "good reason"? If a person has murdered someone, is that a justification for taking his or her life? If one answers, "yes, for the overall good of society," then would it also be permissible to kill a person who is extremely vulgar or rude? Why not? Is abortion—taking the life of an unborn fetus—a case of murder? Is the fact that the mother doesn't want or can't support a child a sufficient reason for having an abortion? Does a society have the right to risk, and possibly sacrifice, a young person's life, perhaps in a war that the person does not understand or accept? Does the same person have the right to risk or take his or her own life for foolish reasons—jumping motorcycles without a crash helmet or jumping off lover's leap because of a temporary depression? What kinds of considerations would lead us to say "no"? To ask any or all of these questions is to force a clarification of the principle summarized in the seemingly simple phrase, "right to life." Such discussions do not in any way imply the rejection of such principles. Rather, they demand their clarification and justification. What do they really mean? What kinds of cases are covered by a principle and which are not? Why do we think that the principle is so important and what goals or principles, if any, might be even more important, for which this one might be compromised or sacrificed?

The more mundane issues of our daily lives are similarly governed by goals, ideals, rules, and principles. In the most general way, we might say that everything we do, from brushing our teeth in the morning to setting the alarm clock at night, is aimed at the goal of "living well." One goal for all of us is, in a word, "happiness." But what is happiness, and what sorts of goals and activities make it possible? Is the good life a single goal—like success or being respected or enjoying oneself or being good to one's family? Or is it a great many things, in which case, how do they all tie together and which take priority? We often talk about "enjoying life" as the best thing, but why, then, do we so admire the person who has "accomplished" something and "done something meaningful" in life, even at the cost of considerable pain and sacrifice? What sorts of achievements are "meaningful"? Is personal satisfaction, the achievement of one's individual goals in life, sufficient? What about friendship, or just being "a good person"? It is often said that *love* is the most meaningful thing in life, but what about love makes it meaningful? Is it the loving or the being loved? Is it the feeling itself, or what we actually do for one another? Is it because love is indeed a "gift of God," or is it simply the fact that, in love, we don't have to go through life alone?

The issues of ethics are the issues of life in human society. We do not just behave according to instinct or impulse. We are taught goals and acquire ideals. We conform to patterns of acceptable social behavior and share in our praise for certain actions (generosity and bravery, for example) and our condemnation of others (utter selfishness and cowardice, for instance). We obey the laws but sometimes disagree with them for reasons that we also agree or disagree about. And however personal and individual we consider our values to be, we agree in our acceptance of certain general principles, not only "the right to life" but the desirability of happiness, the importance of money, sex, success, and love in our lives and the importance of doing the right thing—though we may not always agree on what that is.

In this book, I have not tried to "do" moral philosophy, that is, to present my own opinions and arguments about the kinds of cases just mentioned or about the general principles and theories of ethics. It is not possible to say anything at all about ethics and not betray one's own views and perspective, but I have tried to do so. This book is a text rather than an essay, an introduction to the central questions, concepts, and arguments that continue to appear and reappear throughout the long history of ethics. I have tried to encourage some acquaintance with the history of ethics, although little time will be spent on systematic exposition of the texts and ideas of the great moral philosophers. (I have presented some of these classic texts with an exposition of them in *Morality and the Good Life,* also published by the McGraw-Hill Book Company.) I have tried to present as simply as possible the variety of ethical and moral theories that have been, and still are, defended in ethics. While I have tried to discuss them evenhandedly along with their arguments and objections, it would be a mistake to think of the variety of theories as a "grab bag" or smorgasbord from which each student can pick and choose according to personal taste. Indeed, if there is one overview which has motivated philosophers since Plato in their ethical search, it is the idea that there is a *correct* theory of ethics, that the goals, ideals, rules, and principles governing behavior do form a coherent and comprehensible system, which it is the purpose of ethics to understand. There may be conflict of interests; there may be serious disagreement over what is the right thing to do. The whole history of ethics shows us how much philosophers disagree about ethical theories, but, nevertheless, the reason *why* we disagree, both in particular cases and in the most general philosophical inquiries, is the fact that each of us believes that we are *RIGHT*. Ethics, unlike one's favorite beer, is not just a matter of taste. Accordingly, it is necessary to understand the views we disagree about—and this too is an important part of ethics. But understanding the other side does not mean giving up one's own convictions, and appreciating the variety of ethical theories does not mean that "it's all a matter of opinion."

The aim of the study of ethics and the aim of this book is to help the student think about ethical issues, from the most concrete personal problems ("I promised my 'sweetie' that I wouldn't go out with anyone else while I'm away at college, but then I met. . . .") to the most general ethical questions ("What's wrong with blackmail, if it's an exercise of my freedom of speech?" or "What is happiness, anyhow?") Ethical theories have been formulated to help us think about right conduct in the concrete situations of life, to organize the enormous number of opinions, feelings, and "intuitions" we have about what is right and what is wrong. At the same time, particular personal problems often arise just because of our awareness of the broader ethical questions. A course of action might be singularly promising, so far as our personal ambitions and pleasures are concerned; yet we know so well that this is not enough. Our awareness of the consequences and the significance of our actions adds an additional dimension to our thinking. A student knows that he or she will have a better chance of getting a job with a small fabrication on the résumé; but even if no one will ever find out, what does it *mean* to have lied? A person wants "out" of a tedious marriage because happiness lies elsewhere. But what does it *mean* to abandon a marriage, and what will happen to everyone else involved? Ethics is the unity of concrete human concerns and the awareness of general goals, ideals, rules and principles, and their significance. If we may adapt a phrase from one of the great moral philosophers, Immanuel Kant, we might say that ethics without reference to one's own concrete actions and feelings is empty, but action without ethics is blind.

One of the central themes of this book is the insistence that ethics is virtually never an isolated, individual enterprise. It is a shared effort with many influences, obligations, and debts of gratitude. The same is true of writing about ethics; and my debts to friends, colleagues, and students are in evidence on every one of the following pages. (Any mistakes are theirs too, of course.) Some of the orientation of this book has been influenced by the new "revisions" in classical ethics promoted by Alasdair MacIntyre, William Gass, Frithjof Bergmann, Edmund Pincoffs, and others. The classical substance of the book I digested with the tutelage of Betty Flowers, Charles Stevenson, William Frankena, Julius Moravcsik, and Stuart Hampshire. I owe a very special ethical debt to Lee Bowie and Meredith Michaels of Mount Holyoke College. I have a unique sense of gratitude to my wife, Kristine, for her support and encouragement. And I owe a very unromantic debt to Apple Computers (II plus) for making life so much easier. The concept of this book was developed by Kaye Pace, and the book itself grew to maturity under the watchful eyes of Anne Murphy and David Dunham of the McGraw-Hill Book Company.

I would also like to express my thanks for the many useful comments and suggestions provided by colleagues who reviewed this text during the course of its development, especially to: Thomas Auxter, University of Florida; Fred A. Elliston, Illinois Institute of Technology; Richard Kraut, University of Illinois at Chicago; Joan Price, Mesa Community College; and Paul Woodruff, University of Texas at Austin.

Robert C. Solomon

PART ONE

AN INTRODUCTION TO ETHICS

SMALL CRIMES

Last Thursday, you went out for lunch with an acquaintance from class, a nice-enough fellow but not a candidate for lifelong friendship. As you were wolfing down your last bite of cheeseburger, you suddenly gulped and flushed: you realized that you had forgotten your wallet. You were flat broke. Embarrassed, you entreated your classmate to lend you five dollars, which you would, of course, pay back on Tuesday. Today is Wednesday; you forgot.

Now you are doubly embarrassed, for having had to borrow the money in the first place, for having then forgotten to pay it back when promised. You are tempted, momentarily, to ignore the entire awkward situation, just to assume—what may well be true—that your classmate has forgotten about the loan. (After all, it is only five dollars.) But maybe he hasn't forgotten, or, at least, he'll remember it when he sees you. For an irrational instant, you consider dropping the course, but then you realize that would be ridiculous—the five dollars just isn't that important. It is highly unlikely—it would be very embarrassing for him—that he would actually ask you for the money. Any way, you aren't close friends and don't generally talk to each other. So what's the difference?

But now, small hints of large doubts start interrupting your day. You've made up your mind. You are convinced that no harm will come to you. The fellow knows none of your friends and it is hardly likely that he will announce to the class or put a personal ad in the paper that you are a "deadbeat." And yet, it's ruining your day, and it may well ruin other days. "If only I could get rid of this guilty feeling," you say to yourself. But it is not just a feeling; it is a new and wholly unwelcome sense of who you are. A voice inside of you (sometimes it sounds like your own voice; occasionally it seems to be your mother's) keeps whispering, "deadbeat," "deadbeat" (and worse). Already distracted from your work, you start speculating, "What if we all were to forget about our debts?" Your first response is that you would probably be washing dishes at the Burger Shoppe, since no one would ever lend anyone money and your classmate would never have lent money to you. Your second response to yourself is that "everyone doesn't forget," but this argument doesn't make you feel any better. It reminds you that in a world where most people pay their debts, you are one of the scoundrels who does not. In a final moment of belligerence, you smash your fist on the table and say, in part to yourself and in part to the slightly surprised people sharing your library table, "The only person I have to worry about is me!"

There is an embarrassed silence. Then you walk over to the bank of phones and dial: "Hello, Harris? You remember that five dollars you loaned me?"

WHAT IS ETHICS?

Ethics is that part of philosophy which is concerned with living well, being a good person, doing the right thing, and wanting the right things in life.

The word "ethics" refers both to a discipline—the study of our values and their justification—and to the subject matter of that discipline—the actual values and rules of conduct by which we live. The two meanings merge in the fact that we behave (and misbehave) according to a complex and continually changing set of rules, customs, and expectations; consequently, we are forced to reflect on our conduct and attitudes, to justify and sometimes to revise them.

Why do we need to study ethics as a discipline? Isn't it enough that we *have* ethics, that we do (most of us, most of the time) act according to our values and rules? But part of our ethics is understanding ethics, that is, acting for *reasons* and being able to defend our actions if called upon to do so. It is not enough, after the age of eight or so, simply to do what you are told; it is just as important to know the reason why, and to be able to say no when you think an act is wrong. The study of ethics teaches us to appreciate the overall system of reasons within which having ethics makes sense. Understanding what we are doing and why is just as essential to ethics as the doing itself.

We learn ethics, typically, a piece at a time. Our education begins in childhood with a number of instructions and prohibitions, such as "don't hit your little sister" and "you should share your toys with your friends." The recognition of authority is essential, of course, beginning with "You do what your father says" and culminating in "Because it's the law, that's why." But it is also learning reasons, such as "because if everyone did that, there wouldn't be any left" or "because it will make her unhappy." Ultimately, we learn the specialized language of *morality* and its more abstract reasons for doing or refraining from certain actions, such as "because it is your *duty*" and "because it is *immoral*." By this time we have begun to learn that ethics is not just a varied collection of "do's and don'ts" but a *system* of values and principles which tie together in a reasonable and coherent way in order to make our society and our lives as "civilized" and as happy as possible. The study of ethics is the final step in this process of education—the understanding of that system as such and the way that all our particular values and principles fit into it.

CHANGE, CHOICE, AND "PLURALISM"

Our understanding of ethics is complicated enormously by the fact that, as a living system, our ethics is continually *changing*. Consider, for example, the tremendous changes that our society has experienced over just the past few decades in the realm of sexual morality; today, we accept behavior which would have been wanton immorality fifty years ago (for example, topless beachwear for *men*!). Similar changes have taken place in our concept of personal roles and career options. Only twenty years ago, many people considered it "unethical" for a wife to work except in cases of dire family need, but it was perfectly acceptable—in fact, even commendable—for a husband to spend so much time working at his career that he virtually never saw his children or did anything but work. Today, we would not find such behavior praiseworthy but, rather, akin to a disease—some call it "workaholism." Attitudes toward authority have also changed dramatically. Forty years ago, the attitude of most young men, when drafted into the army (or invited to enlist), was unquestioning acceptance. Today, those who refuse to cooperate and who resist authority are often praised as moral heroes. What this means and whether it is a change for the better or for the worse is one of the most important questions of ethics.

If we continued to accept whatever values we were taught as children, if there were no dramatic ethical changes or disagreements about what is right, the study of ethics might still be desirable, but it would not have any decisive impact on our lives. The fact is, however, that we live in a society filled with change and disagreements, in which each generation is taught to reexamine the values and actions of the older generation, in which doing what you are told or simply conforming to tradition is not necessarily a mark of moral goodness but may be considered cowardice or lack of character. Our ethics, in other words, essentially involves *choice*. In fact, having and permitting individual freedom of choice is itself one of the most noteworthy values of our ethics. But to choose between alternative courses of action or opposed values requires intelligent deliberation and some sense of the reasons why we should choose one rather than another. Each of us must select a career and a way of life. We might "follow in our parents' footsteps" or we might go off on a completely different path. But we must choose. Each of us must decide whether or not to get married, and when and to whom. We must decide whether or not to have children, how many, and how they will be raised, thus affecting the lives of others in the most direct and dramatic sense possible. Every day, each of us decides whether or not to engage in a dozen small crimes and an occasional felony, whether to drive Highway 10 to El Paso at a safe (but illegal) 80 miles per hour, or to take an extra box of paperclips from the office, since "no one will ever miss them."

The importance of choice in ethics is often confused with the idea that we "choose our values." This is misleading. Most of ethics involves decisions between already-established possibilities and already-available reasons, and those we do not choose. A student deciding between joining the Navy or going to law school does indeed have an important choice to make, but the alternatives and their values are provided by the society as a whole. (There must already be a navy to join or a society with a role for lawyers.) One does not choose the alternatives; one chooses among the alternatives.

Nevertheless, there is a sense, defended recently by the French "existentialist" Jean-Paul Sartre, in which each of us "chooses" our values every time we make an ethical decision. By deciding not to take advantage of a loophole in the tax laws, for example, one personally affirms the priority of compliance over individual gain. By acting in one way rather than another, we support one value rather than another, one sense of who we are rather than another. Thus, Sartre also says that we "choose ourselves," that ethics is largely a matter of individual choice and commitment rather than of obedience to already-established authorities.

It is often said that we live in an ethically *pluralist* society. This means that there is no single code of ethics but several different sets of values and rules in a variety of communities or "subcultures." Professional and business people in our society emphasize individual success and mobility; some cultural communities stress the importance of group identity and stable ethnic tradition. Some college and urban communities are notably more "liberal" in their tolerance for eccentricity and deviance than more conservative suburban neighborhoods. Thus, we find our Supreme Court—the ultimate arbiter of laws if not morals—insisting on "community standards" as the test for what is permissible, in the case of pornography, for instance. Many people in our society insist that the ultimate value is individual freedom; others argue that the general welfare is more important, even if it interferes with individual freedom. Some people consider it absolutely wrong to take a human life even if the life in question is that of an unborn zygote or fetus; others do not believe that such a life counts as "human" and should be sacrificed if necessary to the well-being of the mother. None of these differences in ethics is easily reconciled; in fact, they may be unreconcilable. But that makes it all the more important that we understand the nature of these differences, and at least know how to try to reconcile our differences instead of intransigently shouting our views at one another or simply storming out of the room. Trying to be "reasonable" in this sense is much of what ethical discussion and debate are about, and pluralism provides much of the motive. If one isn't clear about the nature and justification of one's own values, he or she won't be in a position to understand the nature and justification of other people's values. And if one doesn't understand other people's values, neither will one understand how they conflict or might be brought into harmony.

ETHICS AND ETHOS

The word "ethics" comes from the Greek word *ethos,* meaning "character" or "custom", and the derivative phrase *ta ethika,* which the philosophers Plato and Aristotle used to describe their own studies of Greek values and ideals. Accordingly, ethics is first of all a concern for individual character, including what we blandly call "being a good person," but it is also a concern for the overall character of an entire society, which is still appropriately called its "ethos." Ethics is participation in, and an understanding of, an ethos, the effort to understand the social rules which govern and limit our behavior, especially those fundamental rules, such as the prohibitions on killing and stealing and the commandments that one should "honor thy parents" and respect the rights of others, which we call *morality.*

The close connection between ethics and social customs ("mores," which shares its etymological root with the word "morality") inevitably raises the question of whether morality is *nothing but* the customs of our particular society, our ethics nothing but the rules of our particular ethos. On the one hand, it is clear that ethics and morality are very closely tied to the laws and the customs of a particular society. Kissing in public and making a profit in a business transaction are considered immoral in some societies, not in others. But, on the other hand, we are firmly convinced that not *all* laws or customs endorsed by an entire society are equally acceptable. The rules of etiquette may be merely a matter of local custom or taste, but the prohibition against cannibalism, for example, seems to have much more universal power and justification than the simple reminder, "That just isn't done around here."

One way of defining *moral* principles—as distinguished from rules for polite behavior or standards of good taste, for example—is to insist that these are not the province of only a particular society or subculture within society but, rather, rules which we apply to all people everywhere and expect them to obey. We might be happy to accept, and even be charmed by, the fact that people in another culture eat food with wooden sticks instead of forks or enjoy music based on quarter tones without a discernible melody. But when we consider a society in which female babies are ritually subjected to painful disfigurement (such as the clitorectomies that are still practiced routinely in many African nations), poets are sent to prison (as in Soviet Russia) or politicians who speak out against the government are murdered (as in the Philippines), these acts cannot be considered cultural curiosities or mere differences in custom. Morality may provide the basic rules of an ethos, but those rules are not limited to that ethos. Morality needs a culture in which to be cultivated, but that does not mean that morality consists of just the rules of that particular culture.

An ethos is that core of attitudes, beliefs, and feelings that gives coherence and vitality to a people (in ancient Greek, an *ethnos,* a word significantly similar to "ethos"). It may be spelled out explicitly in terms of laws, but much of an ethos resides in the hearts and minds of the people, in what they expect of one another and what they expect of themselves, in what they like and dislike, in what they value and disdain, hope and fear. It is an essential part of our ethos, for example, that individual success and "standing out in the crowd" are very important to us, though there is no law or moral principle that commands that this should be so. In some societies, by way of contrast, individual ambitions and eccentricities are unacceptable. "The nail that sticks out is the one that gets hammered down," reads a traditional Japanese proverb. We should not assume that all *ethē* (the plural of "ethos") are the same, even in their most basic values and visions.

MORALITY

Ethics includes the whole range of acceptable social and personal practices, from the rules of "common courtesy" to the institutions that determine the kinds of work we do, the kinds of friends we have, and the ways we relate to both family and strangers. Morality, on the other hand, is something more specific, a subset of ethical rules which are of particular importance. If someone refuses to play fair or to honor a verbal contract, we might say that he or she is untrustworthy or "unethical," but we would not say "immoral." If a person abuses children or poisons his in-laws, however, we may well call such behavior "immoral," thus indicating the seriousness of these violations. Morality consists of the most basic and inviolable rules of a society.

In modern European and American philosophy, "ethics" is often treated as a synonym for "moral philosophy," and philosophers who study ethics are called "moral philosophers." This in itself tells us a great deal about our own ethos and the fact that we tend to be *pluralists* regarding most of the details of life and what counts as an acceptable social or personal practice; as moral philosophers, we are primarily concerned, instead, with those apparently universal rules that apply to everyone without exception and without regard for anyone's particular culture or personality. Accordingly, morality becomes the central concern of ethics, and the discussion of moral principles (such as "thou shalt not kill") comes to define ethics as such. Morality is not the whole of ethics; but one of the central issues in ethics—if not *the* issue—is the special status and nature of moral rules.

What is so distinctive about moral rules and principles? Ethicists have made many suggestions and pointed to a number of distinctive attributes of morality that set it off from other aspects of ethics and ethos. By way of anticipation of our later discussions, here are four of them:

1 Moral rules have great *importance*.

Moral rules, however else they may be characterized, are of indisputable importance. They are like trump cards in certain games, overpowering all other considerations. In our opening example, the *obligation* to repay a loan outweighs purely personal concerns, such as embarrassment and the need for money. Indeed, it is the mark of morality that the amount of money involved is not what is important; "it's the principle of the thing." The obligation would still override self-interest, whether the amount involved were ten cents or a thousand dollars. It is sometimes suggested that moral rules are those without which a society could not survive, or, at least, could not function in what it considers a "civilized" way. For example, how could there be promises or contracts at all—the bases of much of our lives—if the respect for promises and contracts were not more important than a person's personal advantage in breaking them? Furthermore, to call a person or an act "immoral" is to condemn that person or act in the strongest possible terms, just as to say that an issue is a "moral issue" is to say that it is of the utmost urgency.

2 Morality consists of *universal rules*.

Morality is rule-governed in that it tells us what sorts of things to do and not to do, by way of general classes and types of acts, such as "one ought to repay debts." Morality thus consists of obedience to rules rather than just correct action. (A dog can be trained to behave, for instance, but it is doubtful that a dog can be moral.) Furthermore, moral rules are distinguished by the fact that they are *universal:* they apply to everyone everywhere, and without qualification or exception.

3 Moral rules are *rational* and *objective*.

There are *reasons* for acting morally, for example, "because it is my obligation." Morality has been defined by some philosophers as the rules and actions of "a completely rational person." Morality is rational, in part, because it is *disinterested*. A moral rule is disinterested in that it applies regardless of the interests or power or stature of the people to whom it applies. (Think of the classic image of Justice as wearing a blindfold, thus being "blind" to individual interests and the identities of the people who stand before her.) One has an obligation to repay a loan whether or not one needs the money, whether or not repaying the loan will advance one's interests in other ways (for example, making it easier to obtain another loan in the future). Of course, one can sometimes use a moral principle to one's own advantage, but the moral principle itself is formulated to no one's advantage and with no particular person's interests in mind. To insist that morality is independent of "subjective" feelings and interests is to say that morality is *objective*. "Adultery is wrong!" does not mean "I don't like adultery" or "Our society disapproves of adultery"; a moral rule is objective insofar as its correctness is quite distinct from what particular people—or even whole societies—happen to think of it. "What's right is right and what's wrong is wrong." ("Subjectivity," by contrast, is often stated as the idea that morals are only "one's own personal opinion"—nothing more.)

4 Moral rules are concerned with *other people.*

Whatever else it may be, morality is opposed to selfishness. It may be respect for the law or a sense of "duty for duty's sake." It may be compassion or pity or love for other people. But morality essentially involves consideration of interests other than one's own and is thus well summarized in the various versions of the so-called Golden Rule. "Do unto others as you would have them do unto you" is found in almost every ethical system. In the Hebrew Talmud, for example, it is presented as the basic principle of ethics: "What is hurtful to yourself do not to your fellow man; that is the whole of the Torah [the Jewish Scriptures] and the remainder is but commentary." The Confucian *Analects* tell us, "Do not unto others what you would not they should unto you." The Taoist *T'ai Shang Kan Ying Pien* says, "Regard your neighbor's gain as your own gain, and regard your neighbor's loss as your own loss." The Buddha insisted, "Hurt not others with that which pains yourself," and Mohammed commanded (as in the *Analects*), "Do not unto others what you would not they should do unto you." The slight differences among these versions of the rule may make a considerable difference in morals. Consider the difference, for example, between the warning that what you do to others might be done to you in turn and the appeal to compassion, that you should think about other people's feelings in the same way that you think of your own. It is worth noting that most of the versions refer to one's own possible pains and interests. But, at the same time, every version makes reference to the interests of other people, and this is the essence of morality: it presupposes a sense of mutual concern, an awareness of the interests of others as well as of one's own. (The one exception may be the cynical version, "Do unto others before they do unto you.") As a borrower, one must be morally aware of the interests of the lender, and the question, "How would you like it if someone refused to pay you?"—in some sense putting yourself in the other's place—is an essential part of moral thinking.

Somewhere near the beginning of any book on ethics, it is virtually compulsory to introduce the most prominent single philosopher in modern ethics, Immanuel Kant. Kant was a German who wrote at the end of the eighteenth century. In ethics, it is Kant who introduces the most distinctive philosophical version of the Golden Rule; it is also Kant, however, who defends the strictest characterization of morality in the history of ethics. His somewhat technical version of the Golden Rule is, "Act so that the maxim (principle) of your action can be willed as universal law." Kant's thesis is a formal version of the demand we have already stated, that morality is essentially universal and that moral principles are universalizable; moral rules always apply to everyone and never refer to just one person or that person's own interests alone. But where most conceptions of morality at least give equal emphasis to both one's own interests and the interests of others (as in the standard formulations of the Golden Rule), Kant separates self-interest and morality completely; indeed, insofar as an act is based on "inclinations" of any kind (whether personal desires or sympathy for the other fellow), that act is not called "morally worthy." Morality is a law unto itself, "categorical" and independent of all personal interests and inclinations. Accordingly, Kant analyzes morality in terms of what he calls the "categorical imperative." An imperative, of course, is simply a command; morality for Kant consists of rules. "Categorical" is a strong way of insisting on the absolute independence ("autonomy") of moral thinking. According to Kant, morality is thoroughly objective, a product of reason ("practical reason"). A moral principle has nothing to do with personal interest or the particular circumstances of the case. It is thoroughly disinterested, in other words, and it is also what Kant calls "a priori," or "prior to" any particular cases or moral judgments we might make. It is in Kant's ethics, in other words, that the four basic features of morality are brought together into a singularly powerful conception of morality. Many philosophers and readers have challenged this conception, but it is impossible to study ethics without coming to grips with it. Indeed, there are ethicists who would say that the study of ethics is a study of variations in and objections to the theory set out by Kant some two hundred years ago.

ETHICS, ETHOS, AND MORALITY: THE PROBLEM OF RELATIVISM

To understand the ethos and the ethics of various peoples is one of the aims of the science of anthropology. Ethics, however, is something more than this. For example, as the great French anthropologist Claude Levi-Strauss commented in a 1970 interview:

> When I witness certain decisions or modes of behavior in my own society, I am filled with indignation and disgust, whereas if I observe similar behavior in a so-called primitive society, I make no attempt at a value judgment. I try to understand it.

Philosophers often distinguish between *descriptive* statements and *prescriptive* statements; the former tell us what the facts are, but the latter tell us what *ought* to be. It is one thing to describe what people do and what they value; it is something more to enter into their lives and tell them what they ought to do and value. In anthropology, we can and should be content with description. In ethics, however, our descriptions are always mixed with prescriptions, for we are not merely trying to understand ourselves. We are also trying to live well and do what is right to do.

Ethics is not a descriptive science but an active *involvement* in a set of values, a view of life. Moral rules, accordingly, get applied not just to one's own ethos, but to all others as well. When European explorers found out that the natives of the New World practiced human sacrifice, they did not simply note it as an anthropological curiosity; they were horrified (even while the Inquisition was killing people in Europe). When Northerners visited the Southern states during the years preceding the Civil War, they did not see slavery as a quaint custom or a local necessity; they viewed it as the grossest immorality and a pretext for war. When some rural German philosophers visited the sweatshops of London and Manchester at the beginning of the industrial revolution, they were indignant, and they started fomenting a revolution of a very different kind. Karl Marx was among them, and, not surprisingly, he formulated his revolutionary manifesto in the universal vocabulary of morality and justice, as well as in economic terms.

Moral rules are more than mores and customs. Rather, they claim to outline the conditions which *any* society must fulfill, applicable to everyone everywhere. The moral prohibition on incest, according to some influential anthropologists and biologists, is not only a universal moral rule but built right into our genes as well. (Partial evidence for this is the prevalence of incest taboos among most animal species, although such inferences from other species to human morality are always to be made with extreme caution.) The moral rule that "thou shalt not steal" seems to be not just a custom common to many societies but the necessary condition for there being any sense of ownership or public availability of utilities. The moral rule that it is wrong to lie seems to be the precondition of anyone's ever believing anyone else. Imagine visiting a city, for example, where most of the directions you receive are lies. After a short time, you will refuse to listen to any directions at all, knowing the odds against their being correct. A society can exist with *some* lying, of course, but it is impossible to imagine a society in which lies would be more than occasional deceptions, presupposing that most people most of the time tell the truth.

Moral rules are considered to be basic rules because they outline the conditions for the very existence of society. Certain moral rules may be of special importance in particular societies. For example, cheating and plagiarism are considered moral transgressions in a college community because they undermine the existence of a competitive, creative community. Violating a contract and refusing to pay one's bills are considered especially serious violations in business because such acts threaten the very existence of the business community. Some moral rules seem to be of special importance in virtually every society: sexual mores and family relationships, for example, have a profound importance in almost every culture, insofar as having babies and forming families provide the foundation of society. (In a society in which birth control is nearly perfected, it is worth asking whether this age-old connection between sex and morals is still as important as it is in a society where sex is much more likely to lead to pregnancy. Similarly, in a society in which individual interests are often considered at least as important as family ties, in which families are now the smallest possible unit ["nuclear families"], and in which marriages between certain families no longer have the profound social and political significance which they have usually had in most societies, it is important to ask whether the morals of family life have changed accordingly.)

Although morals are basic to the existence of a society, there is clearly at least a shift if not a dramatic change in morals depending on changing social and economic conditions. For instance, the morality of having children changes dramatically in times of serious overpopulation or underpopulation. Whenever the world population seems to be increasing to the breaking point, many people insist that it is "immoral" to have more than two or three children, even when a family can easily afford them. In societies eager to increase their population, on the other hand, *not* having children is typically considered a moral failing. (In underpopulated ancient Rome, for example, pregnancy was so encouraged that there was not even a word for "contraception" [ironically, a term derived from Latin roots].) Indeed, there are overpopulated societies in which even murder is taken less seriously—perhaps permitted in duels, for example, and the death of hundreds of people from starvation is considered merely a normal part of daily life. Or, to take a more agreeable example: In a society in which there is much to be accomplished (for instance, in colonial America), work becomes a virtue—even an "ethic" unto itself—and just lying back and enjoying life is recast as "laziness," a vice.

These variations in morals from society to society have naturally troubled moralists and ethical philosophers who would like to find a single, universal set of standards which lies at the basis of all societies. Some ethicists avoid this problem by restricting their attention to the moral rules and the logic of moral thinking just in their own society, without even attempting to pass judgment on societies other than their own. Other ethicists consider the variations among societies as nothing but variations on a single set of moral rules which are universal. Consider, for example, the various senses of "stealing." Medieval society considered the taking of profits in business transactions a sin ("avarice"), and Marxist societies regard the very institution of private property as a form of theft. ("Property is theft," wrote a nineteenth-century French socialist named Proudhon, who was quoted by Marx.) On Wall Street, it is just another day's business to take an entire company away from its unwilling owners (an "unfriendly acquisition"), so long as the buyer is willing to pay for 51 percent of the stock. In baseball, running unexpectedly from one canvas sack to another counts as "stealing a base," but this is a legitimate part of the game. Stealing a base by actually picking up one of those sacks and running off the field with it, however, is not part of the game and thus illegitimate. There are very different views of what might be called "stealing," but, these ethicists would argue, there is nevertheless an underlying if very complicated universal principle, summarized simply and without the necessary qualifications as "thou shalt not steal," which applies to medieval life and Marxism as well as Wall Street and baseball.

There are other ethicists, however, called *relativists,* who reject this idea that there are universal moral principles, with or without local variations. Relativists argue that morality is indeed *relative* to an ethos and limited to that ethos. "What is moral in India can get a man hanged in France," wrote one eighteenth-century relativist, his conclusion being that morals are nothing but the local customs of a particular community, and nothing else. This conclusion might not upset us, if it meant only that certain customs and mores—eating habits and attitudes toward pets, for example—were different in different societies. Nor would it be especially troublesome if it were only a way of reminding us that *particular* moral rules and actions differ from place to place—whether charging high interest rates counts as "stealing" or whether abortion counts as "murder." What is upsetting is the idea that cold-blooded murder or slavery might be moral, in feudal Japan or ancient Greece, and that we have no right whatever to condemn them.

Relativism in its extreme form claims that there is much more than just superficial differences among societies. It insists that the most basic rules of morality are different too, that not only what counts as murder, for example, but even murder itself has different moral status in different societies. For example, in some cultures, religious sacrifices, such as Agamemnon's slaughter of his daughter and the Aztec annual vivisectionist rituals, were considered legitimate forms of murder. Trying to bridge the cross-cultural gap, one might say that it is not murder in such cases because there was *some reason* for the killing, namely, a religious reason. But this limp suggestion would eliminate as murder virtually all cases of killing except manslaughter (which is not murder) and the very rare cases of intentional murder without any (conscious) reason at all. Or, one might make the purely verbal point that "murder" means "wrongful killing," and thus *all* murder is wrong. But this just moves the question back one step to "killing," and whether killing is always considered wrong. Relativism, consequently, will continue to be one of the most pressing problems in ethics. A society's ethos is partially defined and circumscribed by its morals, but does the ethos alone define and circumscribe morals? Is morality, like etiquette and entertainment, just the product of a particular society, or does it underlie the *ethē* of all societies as their basic foundation? Are we justified in extending our moral principles to people across the world? Or is this, too, just another example of "imperialism," the unwanted imposition of one culture's tastes and standards upon another?

WHY BE MORAL? SELFISHNESS, MOTIVATION, AND JUSTIFICATION

The scope of morality is one of the most difficult issues in ethics; another is its motivation. In our brief discussion of the various aspects of morality, we pointed out that, whatever else it may be, morality is most sharply opposed to mere selfishness. Morality is "disinterested," while selfishness is devoted to immediate self-interest. Morality includes at least some respect for rules and other people's interests, while selfishness is concerned with these only insofar as they further one's own interests. Moral rules have some sort of universality and apply to everyone, but selfishness is distinctively particular, concerned with a single person, oneself. (Matters become curiously complicated when selfishness is turned into pseudo-moral doctrine, as in "everyone *ought* to pursue his or her own self-interest," but let us not get involved with such spurious principles yet.)

This sharp opposition between morality and selfishness leads to the problem of motivation, namely, *if* it is true that people do what they want to do and act according to their interests, then why (for what reason, by virtue of what motive) could or should people ever act *against* their interests, as morality may sometimes require? In our opening example, why should one pay back a debt just because morality insists upon it? An apostle of selfishness might point to our little story and insist that the reason for repaying the debt was not the sense of obligation (which would be a distinctively moral motive) but, rather, the personal pain of guilt and the annoyance of those nagging thoughts. In other words, despite any noble appearances, the act was selfish. Indeed, the apostle might say, *all* actions, no matter how moral or heroic or apparently generous, are motivated by such selfish interests. We may continue to distinguish, the apostle might allow, between moral appearances and selfishness, but we should understand that all actions are ultimately selfish.

The opposition between morality and selfishness has a more dangerous aspect too. In a society that preaches the virtues of "looking out for number one" and "taking care of oneself first," the allure of selfishness becomes more than a perverse theory of moral motivation; it becomes a *rationale* for selfish and immoral behavior as well. In our opening story, this view had its explosive but short-lived expression in the table-bashing declaration, "The only person I have to worry about is me!" But in the competitive world of business and careers, as well as the "all's fair" worlds of love and war, this rationale can lead to outright rejection of moral rules, and the world really does become, in the words of the seventeenth-century philosopher Thomas Hobbes, "a war of all against all," in which life is "nasty, brutish and short." It is a world summarized, too, in a popular version of Darwinism, as a "jungle" in which the only rule is "survival of the fittest."

It is a mistake, however, to present the opposition between morality and selfishness as an inevitable conflict. Most of the time, because of considerations of reputation or the threat of punishment or the "pangs of conscience," our interests coincide with our moral obligations. And indeed, if they did not, we could rearrange society, with more rewards and firmer punishments, in such a way that individual interests would almost always coincide with social and moral principles. This would not eliminate the distinction between morality and selfishness, and we would be right in insisting that the behavior in question, however much in *accordance* with morality, is nonetheless something short of moral behavior. Motivation is an essential ingredient in morality, along with correct action. To borrow Kant's example, a grocer who doesn't cheat his customers just because he is afraid of getting caught cannot be counted as a paragon of virtue. He is concerned only with staying in business.

The motivation of morality thus becomes a key question in ethics, a matter of extreme practical, as well as theoretical, importance. The question of motivation leads quickly into a further, larger question of *justification:* What reasons and arguments can we give for the moral thesis that people ought sometimes to act against their own self-interest? The simple question, "Why be moral?" summarizes both these issues. On the one hand, it is the query, "How is it in my interest to be moral?" On the other hand, it is the more general question of how "ought" type of rules can be rationally supported.

The problem of motivation is a problem of personal goals: What is the connection between a person's own interests and his or her acting morally? Or, is there a distinctive set of moral motives that need have no connection at all with personal interests? The problem of justification, however, has other facets besides. For example, some ethicists have raised the challenge that moral rules, even if they are self-motivating and disinterested, are nevertheless *subjective.* They are just the expressions of one person or one society, projected worldwide for (apparently) nonselfish reasons; but they have no universal or necessary status, no "objectivity." (Thus, the question of justification leads to the problem of relativism.) But again, an ethical theory suggests an unpleasant practical consequence. Suppose a person really believed that moral rules were merely "subjective" and therefore a matter of personal choice. Such a person could well conclude, like the apostle of selfishness, that the only thing that matters is one's own satisfaction, or, perhaps, that "nothing matters." He or she would become an *amoralist* (not necessarily an *immoralist*), a person who acts without regard for generally accepted moral principles. (An immoralist, on the other hand, recognizes those rules but conscientiously disobeys them. Both the amoralist and the immoralist are sometimes joined under the title of "nihilism," the refusal to obey or respect moral rules.)

The question of justification is the question of the ultimate correctness of our moral rules. The quest for justification is partially satisfied—but only partially—by showing that we are in fact motivated to be moral by the right kinds of reasons ("because it is my duty," etc.). The quest for justification of our moral rules can also be encouraged—but only encouraged—by learning that other peoples share our morals, that our morals are in fact universal. (Unfortunately, anthropology is not encouraging on this point.) The difficult question is: What more must the ethicist supply by way of justification, to show that our morals are indeed correct and objective? And if there is no such justification, is the relativist then right by default?

TWO DIMENSIONS OF MORALS: RULES AND VIRTUES

In our discussion of ethics, we have been placing a special emphasis on *morality*. Accordingly, we have so far been emphasizing the importance of moral *principles* in ethics, and, indeed, our entire ethical tradition is built around the importance of formally stated rules, from the Ten Commandments in the Old Testament to the policy of "government by laws, not men," put into law by the framers of the United States Constitution. But this emphasis on principles is not the whole of ethics, and there are many systems of ethics which do not place such stress on principles at all. For example, there are societies where the central concern of ethics is obedience—to a ruler or a religious leader, for example—and general principles of the sort we have been discussing may not enter into their system of ethics. (One could always formulate the principle, "Do whatever he or she says!" but this is a dubious example of a moral principle.) The nature of ethics is also a matter of ethos, and not all ethē are so bound up with what we call morality.

One can imagine, at least, a society in which almost everyone acts in an acceptable way without dependence on any laws or principles at all. Consider a group of children at play, throwing a ball or chasing through the woods. Their game does not necessarily need rules; in fact, one might suggest, they tend to formulate rules for activities only after things have started to get out of hand. (For example, one of the children may decide to sit on the ball and not let the others have it.) A game or a society without rules is not necessarily without goals or standards. The object of a game may be as simple as to keep the ball in motion; the goals of a society may be as complex as the protection and fulfillment of all its citizens. A game has its champion, whom both players and spectators admire; a society will inevitably have its heroes and idols, whom the citizens will emulate. There will be modes of behavior that are unacceptable and punishable, even though no one has ever bothered to prohibit them in a rule. It is sometimes suggested that many social activities work best without formal rules or laws. Thus, business people decry government "regulation" and insist that the business world works best when left to its own nonmoral governance by "supply and demand." And artists often insist that their art consists more in defiance of convention than in obedience to a set of rules. In fact, strict obedience to a set of rules (e.g., in "paint by numbers" paintings) sometimes produces the very worst "art" imaginable.

In our preliminary characterization of morality, we said that many theorists would insist that morality consists of rules, principles, and laws; it is not merely right action but right action *on principle*. If we were to accept this as a characterization of ethics, we would have to conclude that the previous examples of games, societies, and activities without rules are devoid of ethical concern, even though they do have standards of behavior and ideals. In business, for example, there are any number of "implicit" understandings about what is fair and what is not, and a great deal of business goes on by way of verbal agreements and mutual trust and understanding. (This is what is so misleading about the popular characterization of business as "unethical" because it is based solely on the "profit motive." In fact, business is much like a complex game in which the sense of mutual participation and cooperation is presupposed just as much as the much-celebrated spirit of competition.) There is much to ethics that is not necessarily a matter of principle.

We would not want to say that such activities are "amoral"; instead, we are more likely to expand our sense of morals. Or, we might say that morality is not all there is to ethics. The ancient Greeks, for instance, would not have understood our emphasis on rules and principles. They were far more concerned with the *virtues* and the *character* of individuals. Obeying the laws of society was more-or-less taken for granted, but a "good person" was not just someone who obeyed the rules. Such people also displayed personal traits and exceptional abilities, characteristics which involved much more than simply abstaining from evil. (Indeed, a Homeric Greek with many warrior virtues might indulge in a great many evils and nevertheless remain an ethical hero.) Greek ethics turned on individual virtue and heroism more than on obedience and principled behavior.

Largely because of the influence of the great German philosopher Immanuel Kant, however, the emphasis in ethics in the past two hundred years has been on the specific nature of morality as a set of universal principles. But, although we might expect to find rules of some kind in any articulate civilization, it would be a mistake to think of rules alone as the key to ethics. At this point, some philosophers would want to distinguish between "morality," which refers to a very specific institution, and "morals," which refer to any set of characteristics which are highly praised in a society. Thus, we might say with an air of paradox, not all morals are a matter of morality. We can distinguish two bases for ethics. Usually they coincide, but they do provide very different perspectives from which to evaluate human behavior.

1 *Morality* in a strict sense is concern for rules and principles, abstract and disinterested, without reference to particular persons: Of special importance here is the fact that people act according to principles, understand those principles, and act for *the sake* of those principles. Merely acting in *accordance* with morality is not fully moral, and doing the right thing for the wrong reasons isn't moral at all.

2 *Morals* in a more general sense puts an emphasis on character and characteristics of particular individuals rather than on rules and obedience: For example, the *virtues* of compassion, generosity, courage, etc., are an important part of morals, but they do not consist in following rules. Moral behavior in this sense is usually "spontaneous," while morality in the first sense places a premium on being thoughtful and reflective. Morals based on character tend to focus on what is special about a person; morality based on universal and disinterested principles insists on treating everyone the same.

One difference between morality as acting on rational principles and morals in the more general and more personal sense of virtue is this: We might well consider a person moral despite the fact that he or she doesn't pay much attention to the rules, and indeed may not even be able to articulate them. A commander in Vietnam once noticed that his better-educated soldiers, who often invoked moral principles, were also capable of extensive rationalization of some of the most brutal actions of that war. Some of the less-educated common soldiers, however, maintained a perfectly clear sense of which actions they were willing to perform and which ones they were not; they knew unambiguously what situations disgusted them and what behavior was honorable and heroic, despite the fact that they were usually not capable of giving any general characterization of such actions, situations, or behavior. Their morals consisted in their sense of correct behavior, not in deliberations about general moral principles. Of course, Kant would not deny that such behavior is moral; but the emphasis of Kantian morality is on *reasons* for action. Virtue ("aretaic") ethics, however, emphasizes the routine performance of the action itself—even out of unreflective habit or unthinking reflex.

A morality of virtue may be quite opposed to morality based on rules and principles. Morals may transcend the rules. Much of our sense of a "good person" depends more on matters of personal charm and character than on obedience to the rules. Consider the absurdity of a person trying to obey a rule that he or she have a sense of humor, or be spontaneously kind. It would not improve the ambience of a party to order everyone to "have fun." We would not think much of a man who made love to his wife because he felt that it was his "conjugal duty," and we do not think well of parents who are kind to their children just because there is a moral obligation to be so. Moral obedience and personal virtues do not always go hand in hand. Many students find, for example, that the characteristics they admire in their friends are quite different from the characteristics they list as essential to morality.

One problematic consideration is the example of the *rogue*. Some rogues—Robin Hood, for instance—might be morally defended as appealing to a "higher" morality than the laws of the land. But many of the heroes in American movies, for example, have no such thought in mind. They are often out "for a good time" and, perhaps, are a bit crazy. They are frequently chased by the police, and they do such things as wreck cars and rob banks. They even betray their friends, yet they retain our affection because of their charm or humor. (A few examples: Burt Reynolds as "the Bandit," Belmondo or Gere in *Breathless,* James Garner in *The Rockford Files.*) Few moral philosophers discuss this phenomenon, but understanding it is obviously essential to doing ethics in America and Europe today. Why do we idolize the rogue? What does this tell us about morality and our attitude toward it? Is the rogue really immoral, or is our admiration an indication that many people actually accept or at least are attracted to a concept of morals very different from that espoused by preachers and philosophers?

TWO LEVELS OF INQUIRY: NORMATIVE AND METAETHICS

Our various queries about ethics and morality are not all of the same kind. Some questions, such as those exemplified by our opening story, are of the "what should I do?" variety. They are questions of a distinctively practical nature, whether they are quite specific and personal, such as "Is it right to lie in such a situation?" or "Is it moral to have sex before marriage?" or very general, such as the questions "Is it always best to do what is in one's own interest?" or "Under what circumstances should a person intentionally break the law?" The more specific ethical questions are an unavoidable part of everyday life; even the more general questions arise surprisingly often, in particular at those times when we find ourselves in a moral quandary and are trying to find some larger principle or position to which to appeal.

Other questions, however, are more general still, and further away from the realm of practical concern. They are questions *about* the more practical questions of ethics, both particular and general. Thus, over and above all the questions we can ask of the sort "Is this moral?" there is a further question to which we have already devoted some attention: What is morality? Superficially, the questions may look similar, but the latter question is quite different from the former; it asks for the very meaning of the term "morality," which is taken for granted in all the more practical and particular questions. "Is this moral?" asks what we should do; "What is morality?" asks, rather, what we are asking when we ask what we should do.

Because the practical questions ask what we should do, they are sometimes called *normative* (that is, pertaining to a norm or standard of correct behavior). The theoretical questions *about* these practical issues are collectively called *metaethical* questions, or simply *metaethics*. (The Greek word *meta* literally means "after" or "beyond," but is often used by scholars to mean "about" in any investigation or discussion that is about another. Thus, a metalanguage is a language in which one talks about language. "Metaphysics" was the word Aristotle coined to mean "talking about physics.") A typical normative question in ethics is, "Is it ever right to tell a lie?" The metaethical question is, "What does it mean 'to tell a lie'?"

The most common and familiar normative inquiries are relatively specific and, as we said earlier, concerned with the rightness or wrongness of a certain kind of questionable action, such as having an abortion, killing an armed intruder, refusing to register for the military draft, selling faulty merchandise, or not stopping at the scene of an accident when you might possibly be of some aid to the victims. In each of these cases, there is some good reason to fear that the action in question is not acceptable, but yet there are complications that make us not entirely sure of ourselves. For example, both having an abortion and killing an intruder in your home involve intentional killing, which is almost always wrong. But both cases involve extenuating circumstances; in the first, we are not altogether clear about whether or not the victim is indeed a person. In the second case, we can plead self-defense and insist that "it was his life or mine." The third case falls under the general category of refusing to obey the laws of one's country, which, again, is almost always wrong. But in this particular kind of case, what the country is asking is for you to prepare yourself to kill other people intentionally, and it thus runs head on against another moral rule. Selling faulty merchandise would seem to be a case of stealing (or fraud), but what about those cases in which the buyer knows that purchasing a certain item means taking a chance, for example, at a used car lot or an "antique shoppe"? In the final case, you are not responsible for the accident and in all likelihood you would be of no help whatsoever. In fact, your stopping might well slow down genuine help on the way. But then again . . .

In each of these cases, there is a conflict or an uncertainty that forces you to inquire further and seek support for your actions. To do so, you look for some general norm or moral principle, for example, the rule "Killing is *always* wrong" or the assurance that to deceive people is all right (for example, by selling them faulty merchandise), since everybody (in a certain business) does it. By way of supporting our actions, we start to think more and more abstractly, first about kinds of actions, finally about what sorts of actions in general are good or bad. One perhaps might come to the conclusion that an action is good if it helps more people than it hurts, and an action is bad if it hurts more people than it helps. Or, one might conclude that an action is good if it makes society work better, and bad if it does not. An artist might argue that an action is good only if it is original or creative, and bad if it is not. All these arguments are still in the realm of normative ethics; each one is still an attempt to answer such practical questions as What things are good? and What should I do?

At a certain point in such inquiry, however, the very meaning of the terms of ethics comes into question. The arguments we use to support our views must themselves be scrutinized. Suppose someone concludes that an act is good if it is obedient to authority; the question, "What counts as authority?" is bound to intrude. If someone insists that an act is wrong because everyone (else) in the community condemns it, we are impelled to ask whether a majority opinion is always enough to make an act right. Such questions of meaning and justification—the domain of metaethics—lie at the end of normative inquiry. Not surprisingly, virtually every great moral philosopher—and most philosophy students—end up taking a stand on them as well as on the more familiar normative issues. One cannot do ethics, for example, without asking, "Can one *prove* the correctness of one's normative values, or is correctness just a matter of opinion, a personal or perhaps a cultural bias?"—a metaethical question.

When pursuing ethical questions to the end, these two sorts of questions cannot be separated. Normative issues always involve implicit reference to some conception of morals which is their framework, and metaethical issues are vacuous and unresolvable without reference to some already existing ethical context in which they are to be understood. If we pursue our initial loan story far enough, for example, we will get to a point where the whole institution of borrowing money and paying it back comes into question. Our conclusion would depend on both the meaning of such terms as "obligation" and "loan" and the ultimate nature of the institution itself. Both normative and metaethical questions presuppose an ethical context—an ethos—in which they gain their meaning and in which they must be answered. In fact, what philosophers call "metaethical questions" are to a large extent questions about the general framework of an ethical viewpoint, their ethos—questions about the way that people think and talk and justify their actions. But, at the furthest limit, can one question the value of an ethos itself? By appeal to what? One might suggest "human happiness" or "self-fulfillment" or "the good society," but, of course, what counts as "happiness," what the "self" is, and what kind of society is good are all questions that are answered very differently in different *ethē*. At this point, we begin to realize the limits of our abilities and we remind ourselves that ethics makes sense only within an ethos, even if it is also important (within our ethos) to understand the nature of that ethos and its limits.

THE EXAMINED LIFE AND "THE MEANING OF LIFE"

The great philosopher Socrates insisted, long ago, that "the unexamined life is not worth living." That is perhaps an overstatement, since most of us would rather be unreflective animals (our own dogs or cats, preferably) than nothing at all. But what Socrates had in mind was a virtue that we ourselves hold very high—that clarity about ourselves and our ideals which goes under a number of ever-changing popular names, such as "self-awareness," "values clarification," "expanding consciousness," "knowing who you are," or "getting it all together." The examined life involves understanding one's values and looking at them with a critical eye, with an appeal to other, "higher" values. It is an activity we perform every day, when, for example, after forcing ourselves to go to a lecture by some important Somebody, we find that we are glad that we went if only because we feel that we've become ever so slightly "improved" as a result of it. Or, when we walk out of a video arcade, three hours and thirty quarters later, and we feel that we've just "wasted a lot of time and money." Wasted them in comparison to what? By comparison to something else that we think would have been more *worth* doing. And as soon as we ask the question,

What is more worth doing? we are already well into ethical reflection and the examined life.

There is such a thing as thinking too much, pursuing the quest for ultimate justification of one's worth too far. When you are faced with a decision whether or not to get married (let's make it more ethically complicated by supposing that you are already engaged), the importance of careful thinking (before you simply close your eyes and "take the plunge") is fairly obvious. But, in such a case, it is overthinking (or what Sigmund Freud called "intellectualization") to worry excessively about the place of marriage in the history of the world and the many different forms it has taken in one culture or another. Such thoughts are not going to provide reasons or considerations for your decision; they are ways of evading decision. Nevertheless, some sense of the importance and traditional value of marriage is clearly relevant to your decision, which is why marriage is an institution and not a mere matter of romance. But when the abstract and impersonal ethical questions, including metaethical questions, come to eclipse the particular personal and imminently practical questions which set ethics in motion, we have lost sight of our own discipline, and will probably come up empty-handed as well.

This is nowhere more in evidence than in the ultimate question which lies at the end of every ethical system and goes by the formidable title "the meaning of life." There is a sense in which answering that question is the whole purpose of ethics. But there is another sense, which the French-Algerian philosopher Albert Camus calls "a widespread sensitivity of our age," in which the question becomes "What is the meaning of it all?"—a kind of desperate question which invites a most unwelcome answer: "Nothing at all." (Camus calls this "the Absurd.") Both questions are ultimate ones; indeed, at first it is difficult even to see what distinguishes them. But the difference is not in the question, nor is it only in the answer; it lies in the way the question is raised. The first emerges at the end of a long train of ethical thought which is always rooted in the concrete questions, goals, pleasures, and achievements of everyday life. The second is raised in a vacuum, as if we were to remove ourselves from life altogether and tried to look at it "from the outside." Not surprisingly, we get an answer appropriate to a vacuum, namely, "Nothing." The meaning of life is to be found in our ethics (which may include our religious beliefs), or it will not be found at all.

APPENDIX TO PART ONE:
Ten Great Moral Philosophers

Our ethics as well as our ethos is derived from a long tradition, stretching back in history to ancient times. Foremost among the books and authors that have influenced us, of course, are the Bible and its many scribes and speakers. But of nearly equal importance are the mores and opinions of the ancient peoples of Greece and Rome as well as dozens of other ethnic groups whose views on life have slowly evolved into our own.

In philosophy, however, the history of ethics is punctuated, if not actually defined, by a number of truly great moral philosophers who wrote about the mores and morals of their own societies and, at the same time, tried to say something universal about morality and living the good life. Even a survey of the history of ethics would include several dozen such authors, and a detailed study would take many years and include possibly hundreds or thousands of minor moralists, essayists, theologians, social reformers, political theorists, and newspaper editors. But for our purposes here, we will find that several names have repeatedly appeared in our discussion and will continue to do so for the remainder of the book. Accordingly, what follows is a brief introduction to ten of the most influential moral philosophers in Western history:

Plato (and Socrates) Immanuel Kant
Aristotle John Stuart Mill
Saint Augustine Friedrich Nietzsche
Thomas Hobbes Jean-Paul Sartre
David Hume

Plato (and Socrates)

Socrates lived from 470 until 399 B.C. His student Plato lived from 427 to 347 B.C. Most of what we know of Socrates's ethical teachings comes to us through Plato's writings, in which Socrates's conversations or "dialogues" with other Greek philosophers are preserved in vivid, dramatic form. Against the Sophists who taught such pessimistic theses as "all men are selfish" or "there is no such thing as justice," Socrates took a positive and optimistic view and argued that there existed, over and above the changing things of this world, a pure world of "Forms," including the pure Forms of Justice and the Good. Of particular importance is Socrates's insistence on dialogue and debate on "the examined life," as he called it. Socrates spent his life arguing the importance of living virtuously. In his early seventies, he was accused of "corrupting the youth" with his teaching. He was tried and executed by being forced to drink poison hemlock. After his death, Plato established the Academy in Athens for the purpose of continuing Socrates's work.

Aristotle

Aristotle was born in 384 B.C. in northern Greece. His father was the physician of King Philip of Macedonia, and Aristotle later became tutor to the king's son Alexander (soon to become "the Great"). Aristotle studied with Plato for eighteen years, but he also became the world's most accomplished scientist. His theories of biology and physics ruled Western science for almost two thousand years. In ethics, he developed a theory that was very much in the spirit of biology. Everything, including all human activity, he argued, has a purpose, a function, a *telos*. The ultimate human purpose is *happiness,* but happiness is not just a life filled with pleasures and satisfactions. It must also be a rational life, a life in accordance with *reason.* And it must be an active and a virtuous life, "a life of rational activity in accordance with virtue."

Saint Augustine

Augustine was born in Africa in A.D. 354. He was not religious as a young man but, in his thirties, while in Rome, he embraced Christianity and became one of the most influential voices in the development of Christian ethics and theology. Following Plato's and Socrates's vision of the "pure Form of the Good"—which he interpreted as God—Augustine argued that Christian ethics requires the separation of the secular and the divine. In opposition to Aristotle, Augustine insisted that the purpose of life is not happiness, but religious faith and salvation.

Thomas Hobbes

Hobbes was born in England in 1588. He graduated from Oxford University and entered into a lifetime of study in mathematics, philosophy, and science. (He was a friend of Galileo.) His philosophical writings were heavily political and got him into trouble. He escaped to France, but his irreligious writings got him in even more trouble there, and he fled back to England, where he wrote his greatest book, *The Leviathan.* The book is a masterful political treatise in which Hobbes attacks the ancient idea of "the divine right of kings" and replaces it with the radical view that societies are based on a "social contract" between everyone in the society. At the basis of this theory, however, Hobbes also argues his famous thesis that all men are naturally selfish and that, in the "state of nature"—before men enter into the social contract—human life is "nasty, brutish and short," "a war of all against all."

David Hume

Hume was born in Scotland in 1711. He was an atheist and a self-proclaimed "pagan" whose ethics was an attempt to return to the ethics of the Greeks, Aristotle in particular, in which happiness and social "utility" were of the greatest importance. Accordingly, he attacked Christian virtues, such as humility, which he thought to be degrading. He emphasized the importance of having a virtuous *character,* which includes the "natural" feeling or sentiment of *sympathy* and forms the basis of all ethics. He was skeptical about the traditional emphasis on reason in ethics, suggesting that "reason is and ought to be the slave of the passions." Because of his atheism and skepticism, Hume was never able to teach philosophy in the universities, and some of his books were condemned.

Immanuel Kant

Kant was born in eastern Prussia in 1724. He was a pious Lutheran, and his ethical philosophy reflects his Christian sense of morality. The key to his thinking about ethics is that morality is essentially a matter of *practical reason,* and, as such, consists of *universal laws,* or what he calls *categorical imperatives.* Kant rejected both the idea that moral principles can be securely based on human feelings or "sentiments" and the idea that morals may differ from one society or one time to another. Despite his moral conservatism, however, he remained an ardent enthusiast of the French Revolution of 1789, even through its worst years. And in his great philosophical works, especially three monumental books called *Critiques (The Critique of Pure Reason, The*

Critique of Practical Reason, and *The Critique of Judgment),* he set in motion his own powerful revolution in philosophy.

John Stuart Mill

John Stuart Mill was born in 1806 in England. His father, James, was already a famous philosopher who, with legal reformer Jeremy Bentham, founded the ethical movement known as *utilitarianism.* John Stuart Mill became the movement's most articulate and best-known defender. Utilitarianism is essentially the thesis that a "good" act is that which provides for "the greatest good for the greatest number" of people. It is an ethics that, as the name implies, puts its emphasis on the usefulness or "utility" of actions in making people happy, or at least in not making them more miserable. It is an ethics that places far more emphasis on the good or bad *consequences* of an action than it does on the principle according to which it is carried out. Thus, Mill and Kant are often cast as the central opponents in many contemporary arguments in ethics.

Friedrich Nietzsche

Nietzsche was born in 1844 in a small town in Germany. He spent most of his life, however, in Italy and Switzerland, and he liked to call himself a "good European." He was trained in the classics and loved the life of the ancient Greeks, which he compared unflatteringly with nineteenth-century life. Accordingly, his ethical philosophy consists mainly of a virulent attack on Judeo-Christian morality and its religious supports. He proclaimed that "God is dead" and that, given that ominous fact, the morals of our society would soon collapse as well. What we call morality, Nietzsche argued, is in fact just a weapon of the weak that is used to bring everyone to the same level. Unlike most modern moralists, Nietzsche was an unabashed *elitist,* insisting that all people are *not* equal, that some are better than others and deserve the freedom to "follow their own virtues." His ethics, according to his imaginary spokesman Zarathustra, is "for a few," for those who find themselves unhealthily inhibited by the strictures of morality and who have much more to offer the world than mere good citizenship.

Jean-Paul Sartre

Sartre was born in Paris in 1905. He is generally recognized as the definitive spokesperson for the philosophy known as *existentialism,* which he expounded in his mammoth wartime work *Being and Nothingness,* written while he was in a German prison camp. The key to his ethics is the concept of *freedom.* "We are condemned to be free," he writes in his usual dramatic manner. He rejects the idea that our "natural" purpose is happiness, or that we are "naturally" selfish, or that we are "naturally" anything at all. We are what we *make* of ourselves, Sartre argues. By the same reasoning, there are no moral laws or principles of reason which bind us all; our morals are what we *decide* to do, and our principles are those which we *choose* to act upon. In accordance with this philosophy, Sartre was an ardent political reformer, committed to many causes. He died in 1980 at the age of 75.

PART TWO

MORALITY
AND THE GOOD LIFE

WHAT TO LIVE FOR: THE EXAMPLE OF SOCRATES

The Danish religious philosopher Søren Kierkegaard wrote in his journals, when he was a young man of 20 or so, "I want a truth for which I can live and die." He was asking the perhaps ultimate ethical question, What is worth living for? Indeed, this has been the motivating question for almost every great (and not so great) philosopher, the question of the meaning of life, the problem of choosing among a variety of alternatives, some of which (we may not know which) will make our lives fulfilled and admirable, while others will make us miserable and, perhaps, damned or condemned as well.

The most dramatic presentation of this question in the history of philosophy is the dilemma of Socrates. In 399 B.C., he was already an old man over 70, and he had made a considerable reputation (and nuisance) of himself by challenging the assumptions of the politicians and jurymen of Athens. In doing so, he made many enemies and, finally, he was accused of "corrupting the minds" of the young students he was teaching and was sentenced to death. In Plato's dialogue *Apology,* Socrates continues to defend the importance of philosophy, to maintain his political innocence, and to point out the injustice of the charge. (He even suggests to the jury that he really deserves a pension instead of punishment.) The jury is unmoved, however, and Socrates is sent to prison to await his execution.

In prison, Socrates has a chance to escape. His friend Crito comes to him and reports that Socrates's many friends have already lined up a number of crucial bribes and escape routes as well as a safe haven for Socrates in exile. His family and friends will be with him and, still in exceptional health, he will be able to look forward to at least several more years of happiness. But Socrates, in Plato's dialogue *Crito,* produces an argument that has been immensely unsettling to philosophers and philosophy students ever since. The pursuit of happiness and the injustice of the sentence are not enough to justify his escaping, he argues with Crito, who becomes increasingly upset with his stubborn teacher. *Reason* tells him that what he *ought* to do is to stay and be executed; his personal pleasures are not ultimately important, he insists. The injustice of the sentence and the abuse of the law are not grounds for disobeying and rejecting the law itself. One can defy authorities (as Socrates often did), but one is still bound by reason and law.

Socrates's argument begins by insisting that personal considerations—one's emotions and desires—must not determine one's course of action. Reason must do that. Furthermore, Socrates several times rejects Crito's argument that virtually *everyone* thinks that Socrates would be right to escape. "We should not care what people in general [*hoi polloi*] think," he insists. The only consideration is what is *right,* and reason alone will tell us this. And what is right, Socrates goes on to argue, is to act for the good of one's "soul." This means, he argues, to obey the laws of the state even when they are unjust. Not to do so would be to betray oneself, as well as to weaken the power of the laws by making oneself an exception (and thereby encouraging others to do so too). By remaining in Athens, Socrates continues, he has agreed, in effect, to obey its laws, and now he has an *obligation* to continue to do so, even when those laws turn against him. It is doing good itself that is his ultimate concern. Nevertheless, Socrates concludes, in respecting the law he is also doing what is best for himself and everyone else. The best way to live is to be virtuous, even if virtue undermines the pleasures of life or—life itself.

Socrates knew that he had done right and had been treated unfairly by the court. He then faced an unenviable choice: to turn down the offer to escape and face his punishment as a good (if unfairly treated) citizen, or to leave Athens for sanctuary elsewhere and continue to lead his own life with its pleasures and satisfactions. He chose to stay and be executed on the ground that there are matters more important than even life itself. That which is most worth living for may also be worth dying for.

If you had been in Socrates's position, what would you have done? If you decided to escape, how would you defend your decision against someone who accused you of flouting the law? What are the implications of your answer?

THE GOOD LIFE

None of us, in all likelihood, will have to face the awful decision confronting Socrates. But the question, What is worth living for? (or What can I do that is *meaningful*?) is one which we live with every day, whether or not we think about it in just those terms (as we do in an ethics class). Socrates presented moral philosophy with its most disturbing example, but most of ethics has not been the confrontation with death but, rather, the organization of life, the search for the good life, the life well lived. The problem, as Aristotle pointed out a few decades after Socrates' death, is that there are many different conceptions of the good life, and it is not at all obvious which, if any, is the best. For example, there is the life of pleasure, also called *hedonism,* which has often been a primary candidate for the good life. Indeed, when we talk about "living the good life," we typically have in mind the pleasures of good food and entertainment, a stylish house or apartment, a fast car, a lot of money, and the various other enjoyments that accompany wealth in our society. But, even in our very hedonistic and materialistic society, we recognize different *kinds* of pleasures, some of which are more desirable than others. The pleasure of work well done is quite different from the pleasure one gets from sitting in a hot tub. The gluttonous pleasure of stuffing oneself with fast-food hamburgers is one thing; the more ethereal pleasures of reading poetry or listening to Mozart are of quite a different nature. But then, there are a great many goals in our lives which seem not to be aimed at pleasure at all. For example, we have ambitions and want to be successful, and though success may give us pleasure, it is important to see that it does not follow that we want to be successful *in order to* give ourselves pleasure. Indeed, the work required for success at least postpones, if it does not interfere with, the life of pleasure. Furthermore, we fulfill obligations and keep promises without any expectation of pleasurable reward, although a die-hard hedonist would insist that we do so to avoid the painful feelings of conscience, if not punishment as well. We do favors for people without concern for our own pleasures, and we abstain from behavior that we know would give us great pleasure—just because it is wrong or embarrassing. Moreover, there are conceptions of the good life that are antithetical to the life of pleasure. For instance, there is a conception of the good life as the religious life, in which the "pleasures of the body" are to be forgone in favor of the "purity of spirit." The good life is not necessarily the life of pleasure, nor need it include what we sometimes call the "good things in life," if what we mean by this term are simply the material luxuries which do indeed (sometimes) give us much pleasure.

Questions about the good life are attempts to order the variety of concerns of our lives according to some clear sense of priorities. Pleasure is, for most people, an essential ingredient in the good life, but how important should it be? Is it important to enjoy *everything* we do, as we are sometimes told, or are there concerns in life that are far more important than enjoyment? What *kinds* of pleasures are best? John Stuart Mill argued (against his father and his father's friend Jeremy Bentham) that it is the "quality" of pleasure that is important, and that intellectual pleasures are better than mere physical pleasures, even if the latter are much more rapturous than the former. "Better a Socrates dissatisfied than a pig satisfied," he wrote in his pamphlet *Utilitarianism*. But how do we tell which pleasures are of a higher quality? Is enjoying a philosophical argument necessarily better than enjoying a high-scoring game of Pac-Man? Is enjoying a barbecue and beer of lesser quality than sitting down to a formal dinner party? Is enjoying a certain college course as important as learning something in it (even assuming that enjoyment and learning usually go hand in hand)?

Ethics is the study of the good life in the sense that it is the essential effort to understand the order and priority of our values and how they fit together. It is all well and good to insist that life should be a "balance" between work and play, for example—but what counts as a balance? And what counts as work? What counts as play? What if you are enormously talented—in art or music, in law or science, in business or politics—but the fulfillment of your talents and the achievement of your potential success will require a life of "all work and little play"? Is it so wrong for you to "sacrifice yourself"? Or, is this not a sacrifice at all? And if you are modestly talented—enough so that you can be sure of doing *something* with your life but probably nothing great, how do you know when enough is enough, when you've worked too hard or neglected your family or friends? How do you know when you haven't tried hard enough—and are thus wasting your talents? When should you feel that you are missing something in your life? (And what is it that you are missing? It's not always clear.)

Aristotle wrote extensively about the good life and happiness, insisting that the best and happiest life is the life of reason and virtuous activity. As a philosopher, he tended to put extra emphasis on what he called "the contemplative life," the life of thinking, since this is the "highest" activity of man in his way of thinking. Nevertheless, he also insisted that life be full of pleasures and friends, honors and family, not at all the isolated life of a speculative hermit. In fact, there is considerable tension in Aristotle's ethics, between philosophical thought and public action; it is never entirely clear how much the first should be independent of the second. But this only points to a danger that threatens all of us; it is usually easy enough to pick one ingredient of the good life that seems to us more important or "higher" than any of the others—artistic achievement or success or athletic accomplishment, for example. But then it isn't always evident how we are to "fit in" all the other parts of the good life, especially those quiet moments of contemplation or relaxation which are the first to go in a busy life. For Aristotle, the problem was how to be a full-time philosopher and at the same time be a complete human being. For many of us, the problem is how to be dedicated and successful in school or career, good to our families, and, simultaneously, feel satisfied and "fulfilled" in our lives as a whole.

This problem of priorities has increased enormously in the past century or so. We sometimes tend to think of what Aristotle called "the good life for man" as a single universal goal, common to ancient Greeks, medieval Chinese, and modern Americans. But not only circumstances but also goals and values change dramatically, and one novel characteristic of our own circumstances is the *specialization* of our lives, the fact that most of us are expected to do one sort of thing above all and to spend at least half our waking lives doing it. The German poet Friedrich Schiller complained about this "fragmentation" as long ago as the eighteenth century, in the very beginning of the modern industrial age. In the mid-nineteenth century, Schiller's enthusiastic reader Karl Marx was already fantasizing about the time when "man could once again be a fisherman in the morning, a hunter in the afternoon," and no longer be restricted by the narrow specialization of modern life.

The fact is, of course, that specialization is more with us than ever before, and with it comes the vital set of choices faced by every college student: "I can't do everything, so what things should I do?" Ours may well be a life far richer than almost any ever known before, but it is also a life of roads considered but not taken, doors slammed shut, and ordinary experiences untried. This makes ethics an exceptionally important enterprise, for there is a sense in which what we are choosing when we choose a career—whether medicine or business, entertainment or law—is an ethos, a way of life, and a set of goals and values that go with it. Whether or not there are any "right" answers for such personal choices, there is, nevertheless, the necessity of knowing the alternatives.

THE LIMITS OF SATISFACTION

If the search for the good life, whether one tends toward a life of dissolute pleasures or toward a religious life of self-denial and simplicity, were measured by personal satisfaction alone, we could probably dismiss most of ethics as hopelessly "subjective"—matters of personal preference and taste rather than matters of right and wrong. Indeed, where it is simply a matter of personal priorities that is in question, counseling or therapy—or merely a long discussion with a friend—may be all that is required. The fact is, however, that much of what we call "the good life" is not subjective but objective, not just a matter of personal satisfaction but also a part of the ethos of our society and its rules and laws. Even our personal tastes—the desire for a private house in the suburbs rather than a small shared room in the city, the ambition to be rich rather than to be considered unambitious and modest—are determined by the *ethē* in which we have grown up and now find ourselves. We need not deny that personal satisfaction is essential to the good life in order to deny that it is *in itself* the good life. Thus Aristotle insisted that the mere "feeling" of happiness means very little; it is the *fact* of a life well lived that counts.

One way of making this point is to distinguish among different senses of "satisfaction." We all know, for example, that it is possible to satisfy an urgent desire but to emerge unsatisfied ourselves. One might give in to the impulse to devour an enormous, rich dessert but feel bloated and disgusted afterward, or a student might satisfy a desire to join the Navy but soon after enlisting feel dissatisfied with the course his or her life is taking. Furthermore, we can also show that what we satisfy are not simply our own desires and expectations but more impersonal and abstract expectations as well. For instance, if one wants to be an artist, it is not a matter merely of satisfying oneself that one is, after all, an artist; it is also necessary to satisfy the standards of art. (Whether or not these happen to coincide with the judgment of one's peers is a more difficult question.) If one wants to be moral, a "good person," it is not enough to satisfy oneself; one must satisfy the standards of morality (whether or not, again, they coincide with the opinions of one's peers). So, we can distinguish:

1 Satisfying one's desire
2 Satisfying oneself
3 Satisfying a set of impersonal standards, such as moral standards

In Part One of this book, we introduced the antagonism between morality and selfishness as one of the major problems of ethics. We can now become a bit more sophisticated and turn this simple opposition into a spectrum of concerns. There is, first of all, that immediate, sometimes vulgar, display of satisfaction of one's personal desires at the expense, or in neglect, of everyone else, which we call *selfishness*. But there is also the longer-term, more circumspect satisfaction of oneself, which we call *prudence*. Prudence is still a matter of self-interest and self-satisfaction, but it is the satisfaction of *self*, not just the satisfaction of this or that desire. Finally, there is that form of self-satisfaction that includes the satisfaction of impersonal and abstract standards. This is what Aristotle called "the life of virtue" and it is clear that, in this sense, self-satisfaction and morality are not opposed in any way. In fact, the satisfaction of self *includes* morality as its criterion for self-fulfillment.

Aristotle insisted, and we still insist too, that the good life is the happy life, and happiness includes personal satisfaction. But the mere sense of well-being, the satisfaction of one's particular desires, are not enough to constitute happiness, as we find out so easily when we are "incontinent," which Socrates and Aristotle define as giving in to a desire which you know is either wrong or bad for you. Satisfying our immediate desires is not the same as self-satisfaction. Happiness requires prudence—the long range view of our personal well-being—and not mere selfishness. And, paradoxically, prudence includes considerations that may not seem to be in our self-interest at all. There are many levels of self-satisfaction, and there are limits too. Self-satisfaction is not all there is to the good life.

Socrates was seeking the good life, and, by some contemporary accounts (for example, in the Platonic dialogue *Symposium*), he achieved it as much as anyone else. He fulfilled his personal desires (there was very little asceticism or self-denial in ancient Greek ethics). He enjoyed himself immensely. He had many students and admirers in Athens—whatever the harsh judgment of the court. He had a family; he had already lived to a ripe old age in remarkable health. (Some of his friends in the *Symposium* tell of how he walked miles in the snow, barefoot, with soldiers less than a third his age.) And yet, when it came down to the hardest decision of all, Socrates decided to forfeit his life in return for something much more abstract and intangible—what we might call his "honor." Or, we would say that he sacrificed his self-interests for *moral* considerations. Socrates exemplified what he taught—that sometimes the key to the good life may be quite opposed to the satisfaction of our desires and even our survival. Nevertheless, we can say that he satisfied himself in doing what he believed to be right.

WHAT IS MORALITY?

In Part One, we listed four characteristics that distinguish morality from other sets of rules and customs. They are:

1 Moral rules have great *importance.*
2 These rules are *universal.*
3 The emphasis is on their being *rational* and *objective* principles.
4 They are concerned with *other people* and their well-being, not just with one's own selfish interests.

We commented at the time that this list is a much-abbreviated summary of the many attributes of morality that have been singled out for special emphasis. For example, the importance of moral principles can be construed in at least two distinctive and sometimes antagonistic ways: moral principles may be regarded as extremely important because they are necessary for the well-being of a society; or they may be considered to be important in their own right, *even if they do not contribute to the well-being of society.* Consider a nation which is dangerously threatened with overpopulation, in which contraception and abortion are desperately needed to stop the disastrous population growth. If these measures are also believed to be immoral, however, we can see that the society in question has a profound dilemma: Either its members obey the dictates of morality and suffer the deterioration of their society, or they do what is best for society but violate the demands of morality.

The importance of morals in society thus admits of at least two distinct interpretations, one based on the good consequences of morality, the other based on the "trump" status of moral rules. One might also mention a third sense in which morality is of particular importance to a society and which is distinct from either of these. Morals are of *historical* importance to a society. They are a central part of its *tradition.* Indeed, we cannot even imagine our own society without that long history of morals usually summarized as the "Judeo-Christian tradition." Thus understood, morality forms part of the *identity* of a people, and this may be so even if that morality is no longer the most important aspect of daily life or conducive to the well-being of society.

The insistence that moral rules are universal also must be understood in a number of very different ways. This universality might be taken to refer to the fact that moral commands are usually universal in their *form:* that is, they are "categorical." A moral imperative is of the form "Do X!" or "Don't do Y!" Some theorists have pointed out that the distinctive semantics of moral imperatives is to be found not so much in the grammatical form as in the telltale use of the word "ought." Others have said that it is not the language of moral rules that makes them universal but, rather, their application—namely, they apply to everyone. Still other theorists have pointed out that the universality of moral rules is rather to be found in their being accepted all over the world, while others, aware that many societies do not accept all our moral rules, insist, instead, that they *ought* to apply the whole world over.

The idea that morality is rational can be interpreted in several different ways, as we shall see, together with the claims that morality is objective and disinterested. To say that morality is rational is, first of all, to say that morality is based on *reason,* rather than on feelings or personal impulses. Second, to say that morality is a rational enterprise is to say that it is disinterested; it is objective. One's own interests and opinions are not the sole concern. And yet, it would also be irrational to be oblivious to one's own interests. Third, to say that acting morally is rational may also mean that it is prudent and in one's long-term self-interest. Fourth, to say that morality is rational is simply to insist that the dictates of morality are *right.* Finally, to say that morality is rational sometimes means that we are autonomous agents who can decide for ourselves what we ought to do and *justify* our actions, with reasons which are themselves rational and objective. In the sections to follow, we shall see that these different senses of rationality are as often in conflict as they are mutually supportive and complementary.

Finally, the demand that morality is concerned with other people is also a mix of several different demands. Morality may be *altruistic,* that is, concerned with other people's well-being as such, or it may be *reciprocal,* that is, based on the expectation that our goodness to others will be rewarded by like goodness in return. The demand that morality involve concern with others has often been taken as the insistence that a good person is *compassionate* and acts out of *sympathy* with other people, but it is not all so clear how that view is compatible with the more rule-bound views of morality that take moral action to be action based on *principle* rather than on feelings of any kind, no matter how noble the feelings. Finally, the extent to which morality is to be judged on one's *good intentions* or, rather, on the *results* of one's actions is not at all clear. The best of intentions can lead to disaster, while desirable results can sometimes emerge from the most selfish and inconsiderate behavior. (A greedy industrialist might nevertheless make the whole town prosper.)

From the above, we can expand our original list of moral characteristics in the following way:

1 Importance
   a Essential to the well-being of society
   b Power of "trump," overriding all other considerations
   c Essential to the traditions of a culture
2 Universal rules
   a Universal in grammatical form ("Do this!")
   b Universally binding because of the critical word "ought"
   c Universally applicable
   d Universally held
   e *Ought* to be universally held
3 Rational principles
   a Based on reason
   b Disinterested and objective
   c Ultimately prudent
   d The right principles
   e Of an autonomous agent
   f Can be justified
4 Concern with others
   a Concern for others as such (altruism)
   b Compassion or "sympathy"
   c Expectations of reciprocity
   d Concern based on good intentions toward others
   e Actions producing good results for other people.

But it now becomes apparent that we are not analyzing a single phenomenon so much as we are actually presenting very different, even contradictory, views of morality. Thus the analysis of morality becomes a central concern of ethics, and the source of some of its most troublesome problems.

MORALITY AND THE LAW

One easy suggestion, which attempts to bypass the hard search for the basis of morality, is the simple appeal to the laws of the land. This would seem to follow, for example, from our strong emphasis on the importance of ethos, which would, in most societies, include the legal system and the laws it creates. But the laws established by the legal system and the rules of ethics, including moral rules, are not always the same. A society may continue to have laws permitting capital punishment, even when a large number of its citizens consider it to be immoral. Furthermore, laws vary, even whole legal systems vary, from culture to culture; morality, on the other hand, at least makes claims to universality, such that one might well ask whether the laws of a land (including one's own land) in fact conform to universal moral requirements.

Socrates's argument in the dialogue *Crito* includes an unusually strong emphasis on the importance of obeying the law as the key to right action. Most of the time, of course, laws and morals do happily coincide, and to obey rules in one area is to fulfill those of the other as well. But law and morality do not always coincide, and part of what makes Socrates's arguments and decision so difficult is that in his case, the judgment of law is so clearly unfair, even, we might say, immoral. It would seem plausible to argue that it is, *in general,* morally right to obey the law—indeed, one might insist that one *always* has an obligation to obey the law *except when there is an overwhelming reason not to.* But this qualification, even if it applies only rarely, is extremely important. What will *not* count as an "overwhelming reason," of course, will be mere strong personal interest; one is not justified in cheating on the federal income tax (which would be breaking the law) merely on the ground that one really needs the money to buy a new sailboat. But one might well have an overwhelming reason to break a particular law if that law seems to contradict some "higher" principle of morality. (Thus, some pacifists refuse to pay their taxes on the ground that taxes are used to fight wars which they consider immoral.)

What the *Crito* does not give us is a way of understanding possible conflicts between morality and the law. Actually, Plato's view of the "Form of the Good" does provide us with an excellent way of understanding this conflict, but Socrates does not invoke it in Plato's *Crito.* The "Form of the Good," like God, stands above all laws and man-made customs; it therefore provides an absolute standard by which all local laws can be evaluated. For example, many states once had laws allowing slavery and denying even the most basic economic rights to women and children. But the "Form of the Good," one might argue, demands that all people are equal and deserve equal rights. (Plato would not agree with this; the Greeks accepted slavery as "natural" and considered women and children to be clearly inferior to adult males.) But in the United States, it seems clear to many Americans that what is legal is not always moral, and many good citizens are willing to argue that the moral thing to do, when confronting these moral issues, is to break the laws, while also trying to change them.

Morality is not always defined by the law. Many laws have nothing to do with morality, and much of morality is not built into the law. It would be absurd, for example, to try to have a law against, and legally defined punishment for, the breaking of most ordinary promises. Obeying the law—even laws that have little to do with morals (for example, traffic laws)—may itself be morally required, but this obligation must be qualified in the way suggested previously. Legal judgments and even the laws themselves may not be moral, and may even be contrary to morality. People with strong religious beliefs often find the laws of our secular society to be tolerant to the point of immorality, and people with strong liberal views often consider more conservative and restrictive laws immoral. It is even possible for an entire system of laws, and thereby an entire society, to be judged immoral; the familiar example is Hitler's Nazi regime in Germany, which was judged to be immoral in the postwar trials at Nuremberg. Laws must conform to morality; morality does not conform to the laws.

NINE PROBLEMS ABOUT MORALITY

1 The Importance of Moral Rules

There is no question about the importance of moral rules in general and their priority over other concerns most of the time. But, when we say that moral rules are "trump" concerning other principles—namely, that *any* moral rule overrides *any* other consideration, no matter how urgent or otherwise important, we may well be overstating the case. "Thou shalt not kill" is a moral principle of indisputable importance, but it seems that we can find a great many cases in which we are willing to ignore or qualify that principle for some other reason. For example, a great many moralists have allowed that it is permissible to kill a person who is trying to kill you, and many Christian thinkers have defended the concept of the "just" war, that is, a war whose cause is such that killing other persons is allowed. Insofar as the principle is also extended to nonhuman life, it is clear that people kill animals with an alarming lack of moral concern, in order to eat them, to wear their skins, or simply to use them for testing the harmful effects of one or another brand of cosmetics or pharmaceuticals. One might insist that these are not instances in which a moral principal has been overridden but, rather, cases of qualifying it (and still obeying it). But the very notion of "qualification" of a moral principle points to some more important concern that demands the qualification. If "Thou shalt not kill" were really absolute, it would also be unqualifiable. Indeed, Kant sometimes employs the notion of the "categorical" imperative precisely to mark out the *absolute* status of moral principles.

This very strong claim is contradicted, however, by a great many ordinary concerns. We talk of human life as being "invaluable" and "beyond all other values." For example, the idea of buying and selling human life is, to us, intolerable if not incomprehensible. Nevertheless, the very idea of life insurance, to take the most obvious example, includes the need to put a dollar value on an individual life. Furthermore, financial cost is often a factor in the sacrifice of human life. For instance, it was estimated by the Occupational Safety and Health Administration (OSHA) that the lives of several hundred workers in American steel mills could be saved with the addition of a number of very expensive safety features. The cost per life saved, it was calculated, would be approximately 4.5 million dollars. The ailing steel industry did not make the required alterations, but no one really expected it to. We might say that we consider life to be absolute and sacred, but our actions show quite clearly that, though extremely important, life is not an absolute value. How else could we tolerate a transportation system in which 50,000 people are killed every year on our highways?

Moral rules are generally of overriding importance, but they are not always so. A man who is desperately ill but absolutely broke may well be considered correct in stealing medicine necessary for his survival (though it may also be legally necessary to punish him for the theft). A lover who lies to avoid a painful revelation and a fight is not clearly immoral. And there are any number of instances in which one would consider breaking a promise definitely preferable to sacrificing some serious prudential concern: for example, should one miss an important exam because he or she promised to put gas in the car before noon.

Moral rules, as part of a tradition, may also be out of date; they were once extremely significant for the survival of the society, but now they are rituals and rules without a practical function. Taboos are often in this category; they express a once-vital function that is no longer important. Dietary laws often do so; so do sexual mores. Of course, one might continue to assert their moral status as a means of holding a certain culture together through traditional values. But, almost inevitably, such moral rules will be perceived with some skepticism and, in confrontation with other human concerns, sometimes seem less important. Morality, in other words, does not have absolute or "trump" status; though important, moral rules are part of a living network of the concerns of an ethos, and they must continue to justify themselves and make themselves "useful" in the life of a society. In what sense, then, is morality of special importance?

2 The Universality of Moral Rules

We have already anticipated some of the complications raised by the notion of universality. For example, two quite different cultures may judge each other by two incompatible moral rules, each universalizing its rules for everyone else. Such problems have forced some philosophers to seriously alter their conception of universality, such that it applies not to the actual scope of the rules themselves but rather to the *intended* scope of the person or people promulgating the rules. Thus, "Thou shalt not steal" is universal, not in the (dubious) sense that it applies everywhere and to everyone but in the much more limited sense that those who declare "Thou shalt not steal" as a moral rule must *intend* it as universal and *apply* it to everyone, whether or not others apply it to themselves. This idea weakens the purported force of a moral law enormously, however; indeed, in some authors' writings it becomes reduced to the rather limp subjectivist claim, "I approve of this; I urge everyone else to do so as well."

There may well be moral rules that are in fact universal. The prohibition against killing innocent children without a very good reason may be such a universal rule, but notice that (1) the *fact* that it is accepted everywhere does not yet establish the moral claim that it *ought* to be accepted everywhere, which is what the universality of moral principles demands; and (2) even if it is universal in the strong "ought" sense, such a principle can be trivialized (since we have not specified what would count as a "very good reason"), and it tells us very little about the universality of concrete practices and actual ethical rules. It is worth noting that the most controversial moral issues of any given time are not simply the opposition of one moral principle against another, (for example, "abortion is immoral" versus "a woman has a right to her own body") so much as they are confrontations of entire *systems* of moral conceptions, including what counts as a human being, what a right is, and what is most *important* among the various concerns. Indeed, both pro- and anti-abortionists would accept the universality of such principles as "thou shalt not kill human beings" and "a person has a special right to his or her own body." What differs so dramatically are the interpretation and application of these principles. But what this means is that the universal scope of the principle is always modified by the particular concerns, conceptions, and circumstances of an agent or an ethos. So, to insist that moral rules are universal may say much less than one at first supposes. In what sense, then, is it important that moral rules be universal?

3 Rules versus Ethos: How Formal Is Morality?

The Kantian view that morality consists primarily of principles rubs uncomfortably against the view that morality is primarily a matter of social participation, only some of which may be explicable in terms of rules. We will see this antagonism played out in a number of different ways throughout this book, but consider, as an example, the case of a soldier who (as we saw in Part 1) knows quite clearly that an act is wrong even though he is incapable of saying *why* it is wrong or providing any rule or principle prohibiting it. How, then, could he know that it is wrong? By growing up in an ethos, he knows through long experience that certain sorts of actions just *aren't done* and are, furthermore, *immoral*. Does this require a principle? Not really. He has often seen acts of this sort before, and he has even more often heard them described in disgust by his friends and officers whom he respects. Certain acts provide a *paradigm* (a clear cut, central example) of an immoral action, and it is by recognizing this act as an act of that type that he knows it to be immoral. Need there be some implicit or tacit principle involved? No more than we need a principle to recognize a color; we recognize it because of its *resemblance* to paradigms and other examples we already know. An act may seem to us to be "grossly unfair" just because it resembles other grossly unfair acts. An ethos provides the examples and the education. It need not (although it may) provide lessons in the formulation of moral principles as well.

Kant's conception of morality in terms of "categorical imperatives" and principles of a certain *form* leaves too little room for this critical function of an ethos. Indeed, in the strictest version of morality as *acting on principle,* such behavior would not be fully moral. At best, it would be a crude approximation of morality which would be fully moral only if and when the person comes to learn the ratiocinative strategies for deducing such behavior as the consequence of a categorical principle. But how much intelligence is required for morality? Do we put too much emphasis on obedience to principles in our characterization of morality? How much of this thinking is the product of a Judeo-Christian tradition which has its origins in obedience to "the Law" and the Ten Commandments? How important is it to be a "person of principle"? Instead, how important is it (as Aristotle required of his pupils before they even got into his class), to be "brought up right" and to be capable of recognizing the Good and acting on it without deliberation or justification, perhaps even before one learns a single moral principle?

4   Morality as Disinterested

One of the key elements in morality—whether on the basis of principle or any less articulate form of intention—is its *disinterestedness,* the fact that one's own interests are not the (sole) motivation. But, as we have seen, not all motivation by self-interest need be selfish, that is, aimed at one's own interests to the *exclusion* of others' interests. Prudential motivation may well include other people's interests as a part of maximizing one's own interests over the long run. Moreover, satisfying oneself may well involve "being a certain kind of person," which already includes the satisfactions of other people's interests too. Thus, if I pride myself on my generosity, my actions will inevitably include my desire to please others, since that is what I must feel in order to be the sort of person I want to be. To insist that morality be disinterested in *this* sense may be to eliminate as "nonmoral" most of what we consider moral behavior. Indeed, if such concerns are not moral because they still involve self-interest, we begin to wonder what a truly moral act would be. Presumably, it would be some bureaucratic decision in which no one knows who is involved. (The connection between what we call "morality" and bureaucratic society should not be discounted.) Or else it would be that rare act of self-sacrifice—in which even the sacrifice is not self-concerned—in which one not only discounts, but acts against, one's every self-interest. Could there be any such action? In what sense is disinterestedness a desirable feature of our behavior?

5 Morality as Objective

The objectivity of morality is one of the moralists' perennial claims, and the last quarter of this book, on the justification of morality, is essentially about the effort to establish this objectivity as well as rationality. These two characteristics are often treated together and, by many authors, treated as identical; to say that morality is objective—independent of anyone's opinions of its truth—is to say that it is rational, that is, the sort of thing that can be defended by reason alone, without appeal to self-interest or position. The most prevalent, but by no means the most serious, challenge to the objectivity of morality is the sophomoric thesis called "subjectivism." Although it takes many forms, the essence of subjectivism is that "each person has his or her own morality" and, if most of us share values in common, that does not mean that morals are anything more than "matters of personal opinion."

As such, subjectivism can be refuted on a number of grounds, not least because it suggests an abstention from judgment and a freedom from disagreement that are obviously inappropriate in an area where judgments are so often dogmatic and aggressive and controversies so prevalent and explosive. Whatever else it might be, morality is not just "a matter of opinion" nor, like tastes, a matter of personal preference. "*De gustibus non disputandum*" ("there is no disputing over tastes"), says an old Latin proverb. But about moral matters there seems to be enormous room for dispute, even room for war. The most obvious thing about morality is the fact of moral *conflict,* and there cannot be conflict unless something more is at stake than mere "personal opinion."

Subjectivism, however, is not so easily refuted in another form—the form that we have already met as *relativism.* Individual subjectivism contradicts the obvious fact that we *share* most of our values, and we do so not as a matter of coincidence. Morality is not a matter of personal decision but is based on public, established standards. Nevertheless, there is the very real question of whether public and established standards vary significantly from culture to culture, whether the "objectivity" of morals may just be what some philosophers have called the *intersubjectivity* of values—the systematic agreement of everyone *within* a certain society. Even if some moral rules are indeed shared by virtually every society, the fact would remain that morals, in the relativist view, are a function of society. A society may project its ethos as universal values, but there is no "higher" set of principles which every society *ought* to honor.

Some authors (e.g., the Cambridge philosopher Bernard Williams) have attacked relativism on the ground that the relativists quickly find themselves trapped in a contradiction; they cannot say, "One ought to obey the rules of one's own society and not impose one's rules on others," for this would already presume some transsocietal standard, which is what relativism denies. But, of course, a relativist need not make any such claim. Such a person might be satisfied with the simple imperative that "we should obey the laws of our society," thus abstaining from judgment about whether people in general ought to obey the laws of their societies. Or, just as one might universalize a moral principle without its being in fact universal, a relativist might well say, "This is the set of values which *we* accept, and, as such, we will judge everyone else in the world according to them, whether they so judge themselves or not." There are many varieties of subjectivism and relativism which are easily refuted or shown to be inconsistent; it does not follow that they all are. It may be that relativism in some form is unavoidable, but does this undermine morality, as many critics fear? Need a relativist also be an amoralist? Or can an ethics based on an ethos provide us with all the morality that we can possibly need? It is important to have a clear way of thinking about other people's *ethē* (perhaps the most critical question in ethics today), but *within* an ethos—as well as between kindred *ethē*—the objectivity of morals is a given, whatever particular individuals or groups might think. Perhaps the notion of objectivity presents such problems only when we seek to go beyond our ethos and—what is perhaps impossible—suspend ourselves in thin air, outside of every society and every ethos, and try to say something definitive about morality apart from any context whatever. Does this mean that morality is not objective?

6 Morality as Impersonal, as Practical Reason

The idea that morality is essentially disinterested, a matter of reason rather than personal interests, quite naturally gives rise to the suggestion that moral reasoning is essentially detached and impersonal, if not also cold and indifferent to personal needs and feelings. Once again, we are probably dealing with an extreme version of the thesis that morality is a matter of disinterested principle rather than personal interest, including our interests in other people. But it is at the extremes of a thesis that we see most clearly what it emphasizes and what it leaves out. One thing omitted by rational ethics in all its varied forms is an appreciation for the very personal feelings that often motivate us. Consider, for example, the compassionate feelings of pity and sympathy, the respectful sentiments of admiration, adoration, and love, the intimate passions of friendship, family, and romantic love. To be generous out of pity or love is not the same as to be generous because of an abstract principle. Indeed, the nature of an abstract principle is such that it is very difficult to see why one should be generous to one person rather than to another. Why should a wealthy man give his already luxuriously pampered son or daughter money to buy a sports car, when that same amount of money could feed and house a deserving family of four for a year? One powerful ethical principle advises us to do "the greatest good for the greatest number," but does this mean that, faced with the choice between saving one's mother and saving three strangers from a sinking ship, one *ought* to save the three instead of the one? There is an ingredient that is omitted here that in everyday life is essential: action on the basis of *personal concern* rather than on the basis of the principles of practical reason.

Are such actions therefore not moral, or morally inferior to actions on principle? There is probably no conceptual conflict within the Judeo-Christian tradition so dramatic as the antagonism between the conception of Goodness as obedience to "the Law" in the Old Testament and the conception of Goodness as faith and love in the New Testament. Of course, there is nothing in a morality of rational principles that excludes or forbids strong personal feelings of love, pity, and compassion; but, as Kant points out so clearly, these are not to be considered part of morality as such, nor should we expect that moral actions will be motivated by them. And there is nothing in a morality of faith and love that demands disobedience to the law. On the contrary, Saint Paul wrote the Romans that faith and love command obedience. But in both cases, the *priorities* are quite clear, and in our characterization of morality primarily in terms of disinterested motivation, we should be quite critical of the emphasis on rational action in obedience to principle to the exclusion or neglect of personal feelings. But can one command feelings like love? Could one command love "on principle" (as in "love thy neighbor")?

7 The Consequences and the Intentions of Action

"Nothing is good without qualification," writes Kant, "except a *good will*." He means that it is the *intention* behind an action that counts, not its consequences. His argument is that we can be wholly responsible only for what we *try* to do; there are any number of factors in the world which might interfere with our success in doing something, many of which are beyond our control. Kant's view is part of that long tradition in ethics that places the emphasis on one's being a "good person"; being good depends on one's intentions, rather than on good consequences, which may be the result of luck or the most wicked intentions. For example, an evil prime minister, with a lust for ever-greater personal wealth and power, might nevertheless lead the country into a period of unmatched prosperity. The consequences are good, but the intentions are strictly selfish. We might be delighted with our good fortune, but nevertheless not praise the minister. Indeed, we might continue to condemn him or her for the selfish, wicked behavior (though, as a matter of psychological curiosity, we tend not to criticize people very much for their selfishness or wickedness when we are their beneficiaries). Morality is a matter of good intentions, not good consequences. We may want good results, but we praise and criticize the will behind the act.

This emphasis on intentions has been challenged, however. In particular, it has been challenged by John Stuart Mill, who, in his pamphlet *Utilitarianism* attacks Kant's view, asking, Why would we praise a good will, except that a good will usually leads to good consequences? In other words, we praise an act for its consequences first of all, and we praise the intentions of the actor only in a secondary way, to encourage further good consequences. We might note the curiosity, often captured in literature, of a good person who regularly causes disaster through the best-intentioned actions. Perhaps the most developed example of such a character is Dostoevsky's Prince Myshkin in his novel *The Idiot.* Prince Myshkin is a Christ-like soul whom Dostoevsky characterizes as "the perfectly good man," who goes around Russia trying to help people but in fact causes one disaster after another. Kant would agree that he is, indeed, the perfectly good man, but Mill would surely object, "What is good about him?" The dispute is not whether we should look only at intentions or only at consequences, however; it is a question of what we mean by morality, and whether a person's morals are best measured by what he or she *does* or what he or she *wills,* even if it is only in the exceptional case that the doing and the willing are opposed. In such cases, which is more important? Why?

8 Morality as Tradition, Morality as Autonomy

To be moral, Kant tells us, is to appreciate oneself as an *autonomous* being who has the right and the responsibility to decide what is right and what must be done. Indeed, Kant dismisses what he calls "heteronomy" (morals determined by external factors, including the influence of other people) as irrelevant, if not disruptive, to morality. The ideal moral person acts as if he or she were wholly alone in the world—at least, as far as the making of a decision is concerned. The French philosopher Jean-Paul Sartre goes even further. (He says that "freedom," rather than autonomy, is at the heart of human nature, but the meaning is much the same.) Sartre maintains that not only must we consider ourselves wholly alone in the world, independent of any society or culture, when we make moral decisions. He adds that we do not even have the faculty that Kant supposes would allow us to tell, for ourselves, what is right and what is wrong—the faculty of reason. We not only have to decide what to do; we have to determine what is right, with no moral law to appeal to. One might say that the principle of autonomy begins by insisting that we make moral decisions for ourselves, but ends up by making the impossible demand that we make decisions in a total vacuum, with nothing to appeal to, no way of knowing whether we are right or wrong. According to Sartre, we have to *create* our morality, as we go.

The antithesis of this strong notion of autonomy is the concept of an ethos. With the emphasis on morality as rational principles, the erratic ideals and examples of one's moral upbringing seem to be the wrong place to look for a systematic set of values and their justification. Nevertheless, it is within an ethos that we learn our morality and it is on the basis of an ethos that our principles are in any way possible. The Lord may have given Moses "the Law" in the middle of the desert, but nevertheless He gave it to a very particular ("chosen") people in a very particular, if unfortunate, set of circumstances. It is ethos that determines morality, and ethos is the very contrary of autonomy.

Morality is a matter of tradition, not only in the weak sense that we have been practicing morals for many centuries, but in the strong sense that morality is part and parcel of that tradition and incomprehensible without it. A person's "rational autonomy" has very little to do with it; indeed, it comes into play only in cases of moral confusion, and then it is a matter of choosing *within* the strictures of an ethics and not a matter of determining "for oneself" what is right and what is wrong. But then, is one trapped in one's ethos? How is it possible to "think for oneself"—even to reject the values of one's tradition?

9 Is Morality Distinct?

The point of this entire analysis—and of much of the past twenty decades of moral philosophy—has been to determine the distinctive characteristics of morality that set it off from other parts of ethics and ethos. There is an undeniable distinction, for example, between the rules prohibiting killing people and the rules of etiquette, and these differences are surely not just a matter of content (killing versus eating) but something much more, a vast difference in the importance of the rules as well as a complex set of differences in their form and application. It is these differences that we have been discussing, and which we have seen collide so often in the past few pages. But, if we do not take only the extreme examples into account—questions of murder on the one hand and which fork or spoon to use on the other—the distinction becomes much less clear. Is sexual morality, for example, more like questions of life and death or more like etiquette? Why do we call it sexual *morality*? Is there something distinctive about sex which gives it its own moral status, or is it, rather, that moral questions about sexuality are just the same as those general moral issues that appear in all human interactions—questions of honesty and sincerity, the problem of hurting people, and the challenge of doing what is best for all concerned instead of blindly following one's own desires? Indeed, to repeat an old question, could it be that matters of etiquette might be, in some societies, matters of morality? Or, can matters that we consider strictly moral become matters of etiquette? (The example of cannibalism is both too easy and too incomprehensible.) Is morality indeed a distinctive set of principles, etched in stone forever like the Ten Commandments, or might it be that "morality" is a not very precise and constantly changing spotlight which sometimes highlights some values, sometimes others, but has no permanently distinguishing features to set it off from other human concerns?

When we look at specific proposals provided by philosophers to distinguish morality from other parts of ethics and ethos, the results are not obvious. For example, Kant insists that what distinguishes moral principles is their "categorical" form, but the fact that someone utters an unqualified order is clearly not enough to make it a "categorical imperative," a moral principle. When a mother yells to her small son, "Clean up your room!" the order may be unconditional and unchallengeable, but it hardly counts as a principle of morality. What more must be true of it? Kant, in fact, gives us a fairly complex set of tests that moral principles must pass, but not even orthodox Kantians are willing to insist that such tests make no reference to nonmoral matters (for example, the virtue of consistency), or that they make sense outside the context of certain particular interests and concerns. Consequently, at least one modern ethicist, Philippa Foot, has suggested that moral laws are no different from other ethical laws in that they are a system of *hypothetical,* not categorical, imperatives. They all are based on conditions such as *"if* you want to be considered a good person and *if* you want to be consistent," you should obey the laws of morality. In other words, there are no categorical imperatives in any interesting sense.

The distinction between morality and the rest of ethics and ethos also seems to disappear when we consider that range of actions motivated by the desire to be a good person—the desire to be honest, generous, etc., (which is not the same as the desire to be *considered* honest, generous, etc.). In such cases, neither intention nor consequences allow us to distinguish between morality and prudence, for both the satisfacton of one's interests and the well-being of one's beneficiaries belie such contrasts. For this reason, Aristotle does not even mention any distinction between morality and the rest of ethics. (He uses the word translated as "moral" simply to indicate matters of action, as opposed to virtues which are "intellectual.") In his view, there is no privileged set of "trump" principles to be called by that special name. On the other hand, Kant makes the distinctive nature of "morality" the centerpiece of his entire ethics. The difference between these views is not just a matter of theory. It is the difference between two ways of life.

THE PROBLEM OF JUSTIFICATION

The question Why be moral? is a short way of summing up the central quest for *justification* in ethics. To justify an action or a principle is to show that there is *good reason* for it, that there are *better* reasons for it than for any alternatives. To justify quitting college, for example, a student might cite such reasons as "being bored," "wanting to see the world," or "wanting to spend more time with the working class in order to start the Revolution." Such reasons are attempted justifications, and whether or not they succeed depends on whether or not they are also *good* reasons and whether there are *better* reasons for the opposite action of staying in school.

Every attempt to order the various ingredients in the good life requires some sort of justification, some good reasons. But just as we have distinguished between prudence and personal interest on the one hand and morality on the other, we must also distinguish between prudential and personal reasons and moral ones. Prudential and personal reasons, we can quickly surmise, are those which appeal to personal interests and the satisfaction of one's needs and desires (short- or long-term). Moral reasons, like morality, are disinterested and universal; they often take the form of general principles, such as "it's wrong to tell a lie." In the defense of a particular, personal action (for example, quitting school or deciding to get married), prudential and personal reasons are usually adequate, though one might give a moral rather than a personal or prudential reason for even the most personal and particular action. For example, one might say, "I'm quitting college because higher education is selective and elitist and no one should have that kind of advantage over anyone else." Many people marry not just because they "want to" (a distinctively personal reason) but because they feel that couples *ought* to be married (a moral reason). But, in general, particular and personal actions are well enough justified by personal and prudential reasons.

It is different with moral issues. It is not enough to say, about abortion, for instance, that "the idea disgusts me" (a very personal reason); such a moral issue requires moral reasons, perhaps that "it is always wrong to kill innocent life" or "a woman has a right to the use of her own body." Personal and prudential reasons may add to the attractiveness of moral actions by showing that personal interests and moral duties coincide, but personal and prudential reasons do not, in general, *justify* a moral course of action. In other words, in the context of morality, they are not *good reasons* for moral decisions. Moral issues require moral reasons, and moral reasons always have a larger scope than one's personal interests alone. They are the reasons, we might say, that make an action or a person *just*.

The problem of justification becomes much more complicated when it is not a particular moral action or moral principle that is in question but, rather, the whole of morality itself, as in the challenging question, Why be moral? Because it is morality itself that is in question, moral reasons do not seem to work as justifications, as they do with particular moral actions or principles. "Because it is the moral thing to do" is not an adequate answer to the question Why be moral? But it is not altogether clear, either, what kind of an answer would be adequate. At this point, some philosophers throw up their hands and dismiss the question; Cambridge ethicist Bernard Williams, for example, suggests that anyone who would seriously ask such a question must be a sociopath and is not to be taken seriously. But the question does seem to be a serious one if not the most troublesome in ethics. Furthermore, in answering it, we become acutely aware of some very different kinds of reasons as well as the limits of justification.

One perennial kind of answer to the quest for justification, Why be moral? is the return from morality to personal interest and prudence, in other words, to insisting that being moral *ultimately* serves our (long-run) self-interest. For example, if one thinks that the ultimate goal in life is happiness or pleasure (as the hedonists do) one might nevertheless argue that one should (not "ought") to be moral just because being moral ultimately maximizes one's happiness and pleasure in life. Or, one might generalize this justification (as do "utilitarians") and argue that doing good makes the world a better place to live in and ultimately benefits everyone, including oneself. The plausibility of such suggestions lies in the fact that so many of our particular actions and rules are justifiable by straightforward prudential reasons; the rule that one shouldn't drive through red traffic lights is, first of all, based on the very good reason that a person who does so is likely to be killed. But the jump from the justification of such nonmoral particular actions to the justification of morality as such is too facile and leaves out the realm of moral reasons altogether. Perhaps we will ultimately accept a justification of morality in terms of nonmoral prudential reasons, but it will not be so easy. The nature and importance of moral reasons must be appreciated as well.

Many of our actions and rules are justifiable by straightforward social or aesthetic reasons; for example, one doesn't eat chili with one's fingers because such behavior strikes most people with whom one is likely to eat as socially unacceptable and revolting. Very often a social reason consists of little more than "We just don't do it that way here (and if you don't like it, get out)." An aesthetic reason might stop with the insult, "Well, then, you just have bad taste." Some philosophers have suggested that even morality might be defended by such social and aesthetic considerations; for example, much of Aristotle's ethics depends on the appeal to the local ethos and opinions which "all men agree to." The German philosopher Nietzsche sometimes suggested that "one should live one's life as a work of art," thus justifying all actions and principles, including moral actions and principles, by aesthetic reasons. But these two kinds of reasons have generally been rejected by moral philosophers for reasons that we have already mentioned—the universality of morality and the independence of morality from questions of taste and sentiment as well as from personal interests. (One might also argue that aesthetic matters are, like moral matters, not merely concerned with personal or cultural taste but are objective and universal; we will not pursue this suggestion here.)

Moral reasons are something more than social reasons, first because we can override a social reason by showing that it is immoral. (We will not be convinced by a shopkeeper in a foreign country who cheats us and then insists, "That's just the way we do things here.") Second, we expect, by way of a terminus to the justification, something more than a sociological observation. To say that an act is immoral, for example, is to condemn it in the strongest possible terms. We expect that the reasons behind such a condemnation will be equally strong.

THE PLACE OF REASON IN ETHICS

Our discussion of justification and reasons in ethics underscores our insistence that we are concerned not only with doing right but also with doing right because it is right and for the right reasons. It is not enough to be a moral hero if one has only foiled a bank robbery inadvertently (say, by driving through a red light and causing an accident). To do good and to be moral require doing something for reasons and for the right kind of reasons. ("Because I just felt like it" would usually not be such a reason; "Because I believed that it was the right thing to do," while incomplete, would at least be an indication of the right kind of reason.) Thus, some philosophers, Aristotle and Kant, for example, take ethics to be an essentially *rational* enterprise. An act or a principle is justified by virtue of its reasons.

We saw (p. 32) that ethics is a rational enterprise based on at least six quite distinct features of morals: First, it is to insist that morality is based on reason and carried out for reasons. A stronger version of this idea would also make moral action a matter of *deliberation*; that is, one must actually *think* about the reasons for acting beforehand as well as be able to produce such reasons afterward. (Kant seems to accept this strong version, but Aristotle would not.) A somewhat different way of expressing this idea is to say that our behavior is "rule-directed" or based on principles, whether or not one really thinks about those principles before or while one acts. Morality is rational because it is rule-directed. Some of our behavior (perhaps habits, gestures, and feelings) is *non-rational* by this criterion. Morality, by contrast, is *based on reason*.

Second, morality is rational because it is disinterested and objective. To insist that it is disinterested is to insist that one's own interests—and the interests of one's family and friends—are not of sole interest. Everyone's interests count the same, or—in some versions of morality—interests are not essential to morals at all. To say that morality is objective is to say that the correctness of its rules do not depend on our personal opinions. The truth of the rules of morality are given to us just as assuredly as the laws of science—and they can be proven just as conclusively.

Third, to say that ethics is a rational enterprise is to point out that our behavior is "goal-directed" (as well as rule-directed) and is therefore either effective or ineffective in achieving its goals. A familiar way of putting this is to say that our behavior consists of *means* and *ends*; the means or instrument provides the way of achieving the end, or goal. Learning to argue about ethics in a philosophy class can be an excellent means toward the end of getting into law school, while getting into law school may be, in turn, an excellent means to a successful career in politics. A career in the restaurant business, by contrast, is probably not a good means to getting into politics, though it is an admirable means to any number of other ends. On the other hand, if one wants to go to law school, getting arrested for shoplifting is clearly *ir*rational. Not only is it not a means to the end at all; it directly contradicts that end and makes it unlikely if not impossible. Ethics is rational in that it has to do with getting what you want, in the best way possible. In other words, morality is rational because it is also—almost always—*prudential*.

Fourth, to say that ethics is a rational enterprise is to say that not only are some means better for an end than others; some ends are better than others. Thus, it may be true that the best means to becoming an underworld kingpin is to spend a number of years as a professional murderer and terrifying extortionist, but even if this is so, one would question whether it is rational to want to be an underworld kingpin. Some philosophers, for example, David Hume, have questioned whether reason can determine ends as well as means. Given an end, one can "calculate," Hume says, the best way to reach that end. But unless an end is in turn a means to another end (as in taking an ethics course to get into law school to go into politics), there is no such rational way to determine the best end. Other philosophers, however, have insisted that reason can determine the best ends; Aristotle and Kant, for instance, agree on this, though for quite different kinds of reasons. To say that ethics is rational in this sense, therefore, is to insist that some goals are better than others, and the difference among them can itself be defended by reasons that are disinterested, impersonal, and universal. Earlier in this section, we summarized this sense of rationality simply by insisting that moral rules are the *right* rules—dictating correct ends of action in virtually any circumstances.

Reason and rationality have other roles in ethics as well. Fifth, we noted that reason is sometimes linked with the *autonomy* of moral agency, and sixth, rationality also includes the *justification* of moral rules and morality as a whole. These large topics require extensive coverage of their own.

Rationality is often equated with morality. Kant, for example, defines morality as "the dictates of practical reason." Not all rationality is concerned with morals, of course; playing a good game of chess requires rationality but, questions of cheating aside, has little to do with morality. The third sense of rationality—picking the best means to the end—is strictly of only tangential interest in morality, consisting as it does of largely prudential reasons. Morality turns on the first, second, and fourth senses: the first, the reasoned and rule-governed nature of morality, is essential to any characterization of morals that places principles and reasons at the heart of morality. The fourth, the choice of proper ends, is what morality is all about, namely, doing what is *right*—which is to say, doing the best thing. The second, perhaps most importantly for ethics, insists that there really is something true to be studied, that ethics is not just a matter of personal interest or personal opinion. It is the condition of there being any ethics at all.

REASON AND THE PASSIONS

There are many philosophers, however, who have challenged this primary place for reason in ethics. Some have said that reason has its limits and has been overemphasized in ethics. Others have even said that reason has, at best, a secondary place in ethics. David Hume, as we have said, argued that reason is capable only of deliberating means, not ends, and is therefore limited to the third (and least morally relevant) of the six senses of rationality mentioned above. Ethics is not primarily a matter of reason and rationality but, rather, of emotion and "*sentiment*," according to Hume. "Reason is, and ought to be, the slave of the passions," he wrote in his *Treatise of Human Nature* in 1738. One can justify morality in a limited way, Hume argued, by showing how it "pleases" us, but, in the strong sense of rationality required by many philosophers, morality is unjustifiable and irrational. ("It is not irrational," Hume wrote in his *Treatise,* "for me to prefer the destruction the whole world to the scratching of my finger.") Morality is "more properly felt than judg'd of," he concluded; the rules of morality cannot be the product of reason.

To insist that morality is a matter of emotion rather than reason, however, is not clearly to say that morality is irrational. At most, one might say that morality and its ends are *non*rational, that is, not based on or supportable by reason. Thus one might argue that our discomfort at the sight of other people's suffering is not a product of reason or reasoning and cannot, in fact, be defended by reason. One might show that such sympathy is a *precondition* for any moral argument. (This is part of what Hume means when he insists that reason cannot give us ends; only passion can "move" us, and then reason deliberates the means.) But the fact that reason cannot justify our sympathy does not mean that sympathy is *ir*rational. It means only that a good person must already be sympathetic, and if anyone is incapable of sympathy, no amount of reason or reasoning will ever compensate for that incapacity.

To say that morality based on emotions is nonrational may also be misleading, however. Emotions are sometimes irrational; for example, a person may fall in love with an evil, malicious person or get angry at the wrong person or fly into a rage for very bad reasons. On the other hand, emotions are very often perfectly rational, as when one falls in love with the right person or gets angry at the right person at the right time for exactly the right reasons. But the fact that we can speak of "right" and "reasons" here already indicates that emotions may not be nonrational at all, but relatively intelligent human reactions in their own right. Thus Nietzsche, who sometimes called himself an "irrationalist" because of his rejection of (Kantian) practical reason and his celebration of the passions, nevertheless insisted that "every passion has its own quantum of reason." Blaise Pascal, the great scientist and religious thinker, also held a view of morality and religious faith that deemphasized reason and stressed the importance of emotion; "The heart has its reasons," he wrote paradoxically, "which reason may not know." Yet, neither Nietzsche nor Pascal would have argued that one should be *wholly* emotional in matters of ethics. Nietzsche distinguished between the "Apollonian" (calm, rational) part of us and the "Dionysian" (passionate) part of us, but he always emphasized that both were necessary for life. Similarly, Pascal was a passionate Christian believer, but he was also a brilliant scientist and a rigorous thinker; the idea that ethics is just a matter of passion would have struck him as nonsense. For both thinkers, emotion already involves a kind of rationality.

It is Kant, of course, who is the great defender of the primacy of reason in ethics. But it is worth noting with some interest that many of Kant's immediate successors in Germany turned in exactly the opposite direction—in the direction of passion. (Ironically, many of their ideas were derived from Kant's theories.) In general, they called themselves *Romantics* and formed the movement called *Romanticism,* in opposition to the rational *enlightenment* movement represented by Kant. For example, the philosopher G. W. F. Hegel argued for a vision of the cosmos in dynamic, spiritual terms and insisted that "nothing great has ever been done without passion." Another Kant follower, the pessimist Arthur Schopenhauer, also argued that life is not based on reason but on irrational *will,* which is in all of us but, unlike Kant's moral will, has no rational end (thus his pessimism). Schopenhauer's late nineteenth-century admirer, Nietzsche, completed the Romantic movement by arguing, in effect, that what is least rational is the best in us, that what is most rational is the worst—even "anti-life." Life is passion and the good life is passionate. The life of reason, Nietzsche tells us, is a life of pathetic impotence: "Thus it is always—only the emasculated man is the good man."

Romanticism is not always opposed to Enlightenment. For example, Hume, who was self-consciously an Enlightenment philosopher, turned reason against itself to emerge with a philosophy very much like that of some of the Romantics, and Jean-Jacques Rousseau, also an Enlightenment philosopher, placed much of his ethical emphasis on the "sentiments" and thus became one of the patron philosophers of Romanticism. Hegel, we have already mentioned, praised the passions and developed a philosophy that moved through violent conflicts ("dialectic"), but nevertheless, he called it "reason." And yet, the contrast between Romanticism and Enlightenment, between emotion and reason, allows us to appreciate one of the recurrent themes in ethics; it was prevalent in Plato's time and it is with us still. On the one hand, there is the view of ethics and the good life as essentially calm and rational, the careful and cautious calculation of the best means to the right ends, in a world in which things more or less "work out right" for most of us. On the other hand, there is the tragic view of ethics and the good life as sometimes-reckless, always-passionate devotion to love, or God, or the future of society, or the conquest of injustice, which is often contrary to careful and cautious thought and frequently ends in disappointment or disaster.

COMPASSION, LOVE, AND FRIENDSHIP

Whatever the emphasis on reason in morals, there is little argument against the view that the good life has requirements that are not matters of reason. "No one would choose to live without friends," insists Aristotle in his *Ethics,* and it is worth remarking that nearly a fifth of that book is devoted to the nature of friendship as an essential part of the good life, much more than to pleasure or to principles. Kant's morality, by way of contrast, says very little about friendship or the importance of friends, since these are, he would argue, not matters of moral significance, however desirable friends may be for happiness. (We might add that Kant himself had a number of close friends, most of whom did not agree with him philosophically.) The more significant point, however, is the nature of morality itself; cut thin, as in Kant, only matters of principle count as moral; motives of the heart and personal intimacy are of no such importance. But in a larger sense, we might well agree with Hume and Aristotle that these personal attachments are of ultimate importance; indeed, sympathy for strangers and the broader moral outlook are possible only as projections or extensions of these personal concerns. What makes us moral, first of all, is our personal concern for those closest to us. Only secondarily do we learn to have similar concerns—even if based on principles rather than personal attachments—for the many people we have never met and for humanity in general.

Hume and Rousseau both describe these feelings as "natural"; they are unlearned and they exist in everyone, although they can be destroyed by ill-breeding or, according to Rousseau, by the "corruption" of competitive society. The feeling of compassion, literally "feeling with," is, in this sense, the most basic of our social feelings, the basis of all morality and the emotional glue that holds society and, eventually, all humanity together. But the importance of compassion in ethics goes beyond its power to motivate generous and helpful actions; it also indicates what is so suspicious about the harsh dichotomy between morality and selfishness and the arguments that play one off against the other. Compassion, as an emotion, clearly has the power to move us. Indeed, we often act out of compassion without thinking about our behavior at all, leaping to another person's aid on impulse or feeling sorry for someone even before we understand what is wrong. But the point of compassion is always another person's interests and well-being. (It doesn't even make sense to talk about having compassion for oneself, though we do talk—disparagingly—of "self-pity.") But this means that at least some of our most spontaneous behavior is not in any way selfish; it is concerned with another person's well-being and therefore already a candidate for morality. Of course, our apostle of selfishness might come back at this point and argue that, rationally, no one has any reason to act so impulsively for another's benefit. But now the argument is no longer a matter of "always acting selfishly anyway"; it is, rather, a claim to the effect that one *ought* to act selfishly, and this is by no means an easy claim to defend. Compassion, in other words, is more than the glue that holds people together through mutual caring; it is also the conceptual link between one's most spontaneous personal feelings and the other-directed demands of morality.

Compassion, according to Hume and Rousseau, is a sentiment that we feel toward any other person, and not only toward people but also toward animals. It is an abstract emotion, in this sense; it does not play favorites. It does not always distinguish between people we know well and people we hardly know. But the more intimate varieties of compassion, notably the various emotions which we group together as "love," are very particular, sometimes even exclusive. It is possible for a person to feel friendly toward almost everybody, but, for most people, one's "true" friends are few in number, a small, select group of those whom one knows and cares about most. Love is even more specialized, often limited to members of one's own family or intimate group, and "romantic" love (from the same passionate root as Romanticism) is an emotion often described by its limitation to one and only one person, as exemplified in the social institution of marriage.

There is a variety of love, however, that is sometimes said to apply to everyone, everywhere, without discrimination. It is the passion called *agape,* or "Christian love." It is the emotion commanded in the New Testament by Saint Paul, and it is the Love that is sometimes equated with God (as in John 4:16, "God is love"). It is love of particular personalities as much as love of the Divinity in all of us. (Thus, it is often said to be the love of Christ as well.) It is, however, still love, an emotion with a concern for particular people, even if for everyone. Thus we can sense the curious conceptual trouble that Kant feels when he worries about whether the command "love thy neighbor" (Matthew 22:39) should be considered a *moral* command, a "categorical imperative." If love is an emotion, he insists, then it cannot be commanded, for it is not rational and not a matter of Will. So it must be, therefore, a matter of reason, not the emotion of love ("pathological love," he calls it). In more ordinary terms, what bothers Kant is the idea that we can *love* everyone. We can have respect for everyone, but love—passionate love—is quite another matter.

The idea that ethics and morality should be based on love, and that love is the sole basis of the good life, has of course been the center of much of our thinking for centuries. Hundreds of years ago, the poets crooned in France that "love is everything," and only a few years ago, the British rock group, the Beatles, sold several million copies of "All You Need Is Love." As a basis for morality, the view here is a slightly more elevated version of the Hume-Rousseau thesis that all morality is a projection of personal fellow-feeling, now as love instead of compassion. (The ethics of love is often equated with Christianity, but it is clearly intelligible without religion; indeed, many of its most prominent defenders in recent years have been atheists.) In any case, the ethics of love is an extreme form of the insistence that fellow-feeling comes first, with rules and principles—and even ethos—coming after.

Friendship is a variety of love. (The Greeks called it *philia,* in contrast to *eros,* which is something like what we call "romantic love.") Friendship, too, is essential to ethics, but one might suggest that it is not yet essential to morality. Thus Aristotle suggests that we need justice—a key virtue and an essential ingredient in morality—precisely when friendship ends, since there is no need for justice as such between friends. And here we see what might be a crucial division in ethics in a large society (and even in the relatively small Greek city state of 25,000 citizens); fellow-feeling and love will guarantee that at least some, if not most, of our behavior toward those with whom we are close will be beneficent and ethical, whether or not we want to talk of "moral" here (though undoubtedly we can be *im*moral, indeed *most* immoral, to those whom we love). On the other hand, as our bonds of caring and intimacy stretch thinner and thinner until we are dealing with people we don't know and may not like at all, we seem to need some guide beyond our feelings, even beyond those rare saintly feelings of universal respect and agape. This is where morals become morality in the more formal, rule-bound sense, as a set of universal principles which ignore personal connections, ties, and friendships. Thus, in the content of our more personal relationships, formal morality seems abstract and impersonal, cold and even heartless. But in the context of our dealings with strangers in a supermarket or a crowded bus terminal, or in the conscientiously impersonal context of a university or government bureacracy, the ethics of love seems wholly out of place, if not downright disgusting. One might seek some middle ground, such as *respect* (which Kant suggested, unsure whether this is a function of "feeling" or practical reason), but this too seems a bit aloof and distant for our more intimate relationships, and perhaps a bit too warm and personal for our bureaucratic encounters.

There is certainly no sharp division between the personal and the impersonal domains of morals. Our lives are filled with "acquaintances" and colleagues who are neither clearly friends nor strangers. Ethics is thus an amalgam, too, of personal impulses and obedience to rules, and we are acutely sensitive to what seem to be uncomfortable mixtures of the two. We react suspiciously when a mere acquaintance gets "too friendly" and we are offended when a friend even says "hello" a bit too aloofly. In other societies, even the language dictates such differences (for example, the distinction between *du* and *Sie* in German, or *tu* and *Usted* in Spanish, or the ending *san* and its many variations in Japanese). Indeed, in some societies (not ours), such concepts of "distance" would be the central category of ethics, more important than equality or agape or the categorical imperative.

A MATTER OF MOTIVES

Those who consider morality to consist mainly of obedience to rules—Immanuel Kant, for instance—and those who insist that there be a more personal and passionate element in morals—Hume's "sympathy," for example—share at least one basic assumption about morality: Moral behavior depends not only on a person's actions and their effects but also on the *motives* of action. Kant begins his moral philosophy by insisting that "the only thing that is good without qualification is a *good will,*" that is, the right intentions. One can foul up in any number of ways; the circumstances may make success impossible. But it is the *intention* and the *effort* that count at least as much as the results. For Hume, on the other hand, a person is judged to be a good person in part because of his or her *character,* or, in other words, those sentiments that serve as the springs of action. A good person is one who is moved to act in the right ways by the right feelings, especially such feelings as justice, kindness, and sympathy.

Not all moral philosophers have accepted this emphasis on motives. John Stuart Mill, for example, distinguishes between a good *person* and a good *act* and insists that we have very different ways of evaluating them. We might judge a person on the basis of his or her motives, Mill says, but we judge an action simply in terms of its *consequences.* Indeed, he asks, why would we even value good intentions and feelings at all, except that they, in general, lead to good results? As we shall see in Part Four, this debate between moralists who emphasize intentions and feelings on the one hand, and consequences on the other, has elevated into one of the primary disputes in contemporary ethics. Most prominent is the ongoing debate between those who follow Kant in his insistence on respect for and obedience to rules ("acting for the sake of one's duty") and those who follow Mill and the utilitarians in insisting that it is primarily the good and bad consequences that count in moral theory.

This emphasis on motivation has two edges, however; what we have just emphasized tends to ennoble ethics by making moral behavior not merely a matter of correct behavior, which might just as well be obtained by conditioning or obedience training, but a matter of the honorable motives behind that behavior. The emphasis here, quite naturally, is on those more estimable intentions, such as "wanting to do one's duty" and "showing respect for the law" and our more benign feelings, such as sympathy, love, and fellow-feeling. But suppose the "springs of action" were not so noble and the motives for morality were not so much concerned with duty and fellow-feeling. Suppose the dominant motive for morality were *fear.* What would we say about morality then? And would we still feel, as we now do, that morality ought to have "trump" status among our various rules and principles?

This drastic challenge to morality has always been around. Socrates had to argue against it in the early books of Plato's *Republic*; Saint Augustine was painfully aware of its possibility. But the thinker who is most responsible for elevating this suspicion about morality to a full-blown philosophy is Friedrich Nietzsche. Morals, he argued at the end of the last century, are not motivated by duty or respect or love or sympathy; they are motivated by fear, envy, and resentment. Much of traditional morality, he pointed out, has been motivated by the hardly honorable emotion of sheer terror—of one's masters, of the king, and, most of all, of God. Millions may have walked "the straight and narrow" in order to avoid the everlasting flames of Hell, but that scarcely entitles them to any claim to nobility. Action for the sake of duty may be honorable, but action based on fear is, rather, the mark of cowardice.

It is not fear that Nietzsche cites as the most vicious motive of morality, however. Indeed, fear at least is straightforward and usually doesn't pretend to be more than it is. It is otherwise with those virulent motives of envy and resentment, both of which are vengeful emotions. Indeed, Nietzsche sometimes characterizes morality itself as "the greatest act of revenge in history." Revenge for whom? And against whom? Nietzsche tells us that it is the revenge of the weak against the strong, of the losers against the winners, of the slaves against their masters. The commandments of morality consist of prohibitions against the strong for the protection of the weak. Why else, Nietzsche suggests, would so many of our moral principles be *negative*, "Thou shalt not . . ."? How else can one interpret such promises as "the meek shall inherit the earth" and "it is easier for a camel to pass through the eye of a needle than for a rich man to enter the Kingdom of Heaven"? These are the expressions of envy and resentment, the bitterness of those who do not have power, wealth, and earthly glory against those who do have them. Morality, Nietzsche concludes, is not the noble aspect of our lives that we have pretended; it is an expression of weakness and therefore ignoble and hypocritical, pretending to be something that it is not.

Nietzsche's attack on morality forces us to distinguish, more than we have done before, between the *motivation* and *justification* of an action. The motivation is what moves us to act; the justification is what makes that act *right*. Often, in the history of morals, people have insisted that good motivation guarantees right action; indeed, Plato and Aristotle even insist that it is *impossible* for a person to know what the good is and not to act on it. But Nietzsche's challenge raises the question of whether moral behavior motivated (or partially motivated) by insidious motives can still be considered good. Nietzsche does not attack the justifiability of morality as much as he denies its noble motivation. Indeed, even Kant, the champion of morality, admits that some of the motives for our actions will forever be unknown to us (German philosophers were arguing this more than century before Freud). But does this lack of knowledge undermine morality? Or should we perhaps say that some motives, even when present and powerful, are irrelevant to morality?

EGOISM AND ALTRUISM

In the general debate about motives and morality, two general categories of motives loom above all the rest. They are the categories of *egoism* and *altruism*. Like most moral categories, these are also used to refer to the consequences, as well as the motivation, of action. (Many biologists have recently been using the words "egoism" and "altruism" to refer to the behavior of genes and insects, for example, where the question of motive cannot intelligibly arise.) The contrast between egoism and altruism is related, but not identical, to the contrast between prudence and morality. Egoism, like prudence, means looking out for your own interests (though the word "egoism," unlike "pru-dence," suggests some essential antagonism between one's own interests and the interests of others). Altruism, however, means acting for the interests of others. We have already noted that morality (though often confused with altru-ism) may be concerned primarily with principles rather than with the interests of others. Altruism, on the other hand, is precisely this concern for the interests of other people. It may be based on some sense of attachment or compassion, but it need not be. (One could be altruistic on principle, though this might still be distinguished from morality. Consider, for example, a man who is routinely altruistic just because he thinks of himself as worthless and of other people's interests as more important than his own.)

On the one hand, egoism is obviously antithetical to morality; it designates concern for one's own interests whatever the rules and whatever one's obliga-tions. (One can, of course, be moral and fulfill one's obligations just as a means to satisfying one's interests, but this is a complication we can postpone until later.) On the other hand, egoism, many ethicists have argued, is the sole basis for *any* human behavior, moral or otherwise. This raises a very difficult ques-tion: If this is true, how is it possible ever to act for the sake of others (unless their interests coincide with our own) or for the sake of morality (unless our obligations also satisfy our interests)? Are we moral (when we are moral) only because being so is in our interests? If I give money to a beggar and feel good that I have done so, have I in fact given him the money only in order to feel good afterward?

Philosophers sometimes distinguish between psychological egoism and eth-ical egoism. *Psychological egoism* is the psychological theory that everything that we do, we do for our own interests, whether or not the same act serves other people's interests or moral obligations. *Ethical egoism* is the view that one *ought* to act in one's own interests. Of course, if psychological egoism is true, one cannot help but act in one's own interests. Nevertheless, the two posi-tions are distinct. One might believe that all people are motivated by their own interests and nevertheless try to make sure that these interests coincide with the common good and morality (for example, by inflicting punishment to offset any personal advantage in wrongdoing). And one might well believe that peo-ple are not "naturally" out for their own interests but that they *ought* to be so. Imagine a person who believes, for instance, that most of the damage done in the world is caused by "do-gooders" who "ought to mind their own business." Egoism, by contrast, might seem like virtue.

Altruism might also be divided into two parts: psychological altruism, the theory that people "naturally" act for the benefit of others—and ethical altru-ism, the view that they *ought* to act for the benefit of others. Many theorists have debated whether *any* of our actions are altruistically motivated, but very few have ever asserted that *all* of them are. The debate, therefore, centers on psychological egoism and the question of whether all our actions are self-interested. Ethical altruism quite naturally runs into questions about morality, and although the two concepts are different, the questions raised about their justification, for example, are essentially the same. The questions, "Why should I be moral?" and "Why should I care about anyone else?" are generally tackled together, and for most practical purposes, they receive much the same set of answers.

A NOTE ON SELFISHNESS

According to a popular story, President Lincoln was passing a puddle in a carriage when he saw that several piglets were drowning as the mother pig squealed helplessly. He stopped the carriage and saved the piglets. (Whether the mother pig thanked him was not recorded.) Back on the road, Lincoln's companion asked him whether that act counted as a pure case of altruism; Lincoln replied, "Why, that was the very essence of selfishness. I should have had no peace of mind all day."

The word "egoism," unlike the word "prudence," suggests some antagonism between one's own interests and the interests of others. Nevertheless, one can be an egoist and also be charming, morally correct, and even a philanthropist, as a number of very wealthy and ambitious people have demonstrated. The word "selfishness," however, is another matter. "Selfishness" has built into it the antagonism between one's own and others' interests, and to say that someone is selfish is to say that this person not only is an egoist but also that he or she subverts the interests of others. "Selfishness" has an undeniable connotation of condemnation and should not be confused with the more neutral terms "egoism" and "prudence." To suggest that everyone's behavior is motivated by prudence or by self-interest is at least a plausible hypothesis; to suggest that everyone's behavior is selfish is both offensive and implausible (though nevertheless there are terrible times when it appears to be true). Accordingly, Lincoln's reply to his friend seems like nonsense. Satisfying oneself is not the same as being selfish.

WHY BE REASONABLE?

Our discussion of motives and morals, egoism and altruism, coupled with our contrast between reason and passion, may well provoke the question, *Why?* — not only "Why be moral?" (to which we will return at length in Part Four), but also the question, "But why be reasonable?" Indeed, the first question has often been answered (for example, by Kant and many of his followers) in terms of the second; that is, one *ought* to be moral simply because one is a *rational* being. And so the question confronts us, "Why be rational?" It must be said that the usual philosophical reply to this, which goes back at least to Aristotle, is less than convincing. It is: If you care enough to ask the question, then you have already proven yourself to be rational. And if you won't ask the question and insist on being irrational, then what kind of answer could possibly satisfy you?

This long-established answer simply will not do. First of all, it ignores the several different meanings of "rationality." Second, it misses the point of the question that is actually being asked. We previously distinguished several different senses in which morality is a rational enterprise: It is based on reason and consists of principles; it is disinterested and objective. It leads, it is to be hoped, to one's own ultimate well-being, but it is also concerned—essentially concerned—with other people and their interests. Which of these is in question here? Are *any* of them in question?

There is a more general sense of "rational," however, which is other than the several senses already mentioned. "Rational" in this broader sense is used in the too-quick reply to the question, Why be rational? We sometimes use "rational" simply to describe anyone who asks articulate questions and expects intelligible answers, whether they have to do with morality or science or any other human endeavor. In this sense, people who ask, "Why be rational?" are indeed proving themselves to be rational, but not in the sense they are asking *about*. For example, someone may be asking, "Why respect abstract principles, unless they also make life better for people?" Or, the questioner may be asking, "Why should I act disinterestedly? Why not give special treatment to my friends and family and other people I like?" Or, he or she may be asking a straightforward prudential question, "Why should I act in any way that is not in my own self-interest?" In any of these three cases, pointing out that the person doing the asking is already an articulate and reason-seeking being does nothing to answer the question being asked.

The rationality of ethics is a set of claims about moral principles, not a single, unambiguous feature of morality. But in everyday life, the question, Why be rational? has yet another meaning, which might help us understand the motivation behind these others. Consider the more ordinary challenge, Why be reasonable? Here we know what is being asked; it is not only the challenge of prudence to morals by way of, Why should I not act in my own self-interest? It is also a split within prudence itself. A person knows that cigarette smoking causes lung cancer and has already developed a suspicious cough. Yet, he or she refuses to stop smoking, not because of being unable to do so, but simply because of wanting to smoke. "Is it reasonable to sacrifice ten or twenty years of life and health for a daily pack of cigarettes?" Well, if you think of it that way, certainly not. But then, the smoker goes on to ask rhetorically, "Why should I be reasonable?" What is in question, in other words, is the very idea of long-term, reflective evaluation. Immediate gratification and doing what one wants to do eclipse any demand that is not immediate or based on one's present desires or impulses—including many moral duties, but not limited to them. The question, Why be reasonable? is thus a general attack on ethics as a whole.

One might answer the smoker by pointing out the excruciating pain of certain moments in the future. Indeed, an effective, if revolting, way of discouraging some people from smoking is to force them to meet patients suffering from terminal lung cancer, precisely in order to make those abstract future moments immediately visible to them. Similarly, one teaches morality, in part, by pointing out the pains and punishments which will in all likelihood follow, if not now, then in the indefinite future. It is suggested, for example, that bad habits, once formed, are hard to change and will, sooner or later, cause one severe social discomfort or worse. Thus one response to the question, Why be reasonable? is to make future results seem more immediate, so that the impulses of the moment are not so overwhelming.

This is not, of course, a philosophical answer; it in no way *justifies* being reasonable. It only *motivates* a person to do what is reasonable. All of us are to some extent caught up in the present and blind or neglectful of the future. (Some people are so obsessed with the future that they are blind or neglectful of the present, but let us not worry about their brand of unreasonableness here.) To be reasonable is to see beyond the present and to take into consideration more general concerns than our own immediate impulses. However difficult it may be to appreciate when we are caught up in an immediate desire, the simple fact is that there are any number of satisfactions in life that are thwarted by impulses which may also endanger life itself.

Earlier, we introduced the concept of an *end,* a goal. Coupled with ends are *means*—our instruments and techniques for reaching those goals. Going to law school is a means to the end of being a lawyer. Lending your textbook to a friend may be a means to the end of having a perfect excuse not to study. Sometimes, means may become ends themselves—for example, for the law student who enjoys law school to the point of wanting to keep on attending classes indefinitely. Often, ends are also means—for example, wanting to be a lawyer in order to fight for justice for an oppressed minority. But this shows that ends and means are not discrete chunks of life, isolated goals coupled with a number of limited means whose only purpose is to satisfy those ends. Our ends and means form a complex network, in which acting on immediate, isolated impulses often tears the fabric of our lives as a whole, satisfying a particular desire but, unfortunately, causing us to be deeply dissatisfied.

Here, then, is one way of answering the question, Why be reasonable? and with it, some of the more sophisticated senses of the question, Why be rational? On the assumption that a person cares about what happens in the future as well as in the present and in some sense considers future moments to be as (potentially) real as present moments, acting reasonably or rationally is nothing less than trying to get what one *really* wants, which is not just momentary satisfaction but a satisfying life. This is obviously true of prudence in cases when satisfaction of a short-term impulse, such as trying to jump a motorcycle over a barrel, may well curtail a great many longer-term impulses. It is also true of all those major fibers that tie our lives together—friends, family, careers—which are not contained in moments and must be cultivated and developed over years and years, which can be destroyed in a single foolish moment. It also goes some way to answering the specific question, Why be moral? insofar as being moral, at least much of the time, is also the mode of behavior most likely to be conducive to getting what we want out of life— maintaining the respect of our friends and the trust of our acquaintances as well as avoiding the unpleasant, unending machinations of a life lived in the shadows of deception. This is not the whole story, of course, for it is only a prudential motive for morality, not a justification as such. And, it probably will not work all the time. Nevertheless, it goes a long way in providing an initial answer to the general set of questions, Why be rational? And that answer is this: Being rational is nothing less than maximizing one's chances for happiness and getting what one really wants out of life. Most of the time, that is more than sufficient.

In the complex continuum of ends and means that make up the fabric of our lives, certain fibers seem to be more than mere threads in the pattern; pressed to say what further ends they might serve, we find ourselves at a loss for words, or going in tight little circles. Philosophers call these apparently terminal ends *intrinsic goods* or *ends in themselves*. Some prominent candidates have been pleasure, happiness, friendship, love, and knowledge. If asked why one wants pleasure, for example, it would be hard to formulate an adequate answer. "Because I enjoy it," is surely circular, and to say, "It makes me happy," is either ambiguous or false (since there is much more to happiness than pleasure). A different way of answering the question, Why be rational? might be put in terms of intrinsic goods or ends in themselves: To be rational is to strive for ends in themselves and not to sacrifice these ends to lesser ends which are not intrinsic goods. For example, if one studies a subject to gain knowledge (an intrinsic good), it is irrational to study in such a way—perhaps in order to get good grades on a test—that one learns less rather than more, or worse, is "turned off" the subject altogether. Morality, we can now say, is also a candidate, if not one of the essential candidates, for an intrinsic good. To act morally is not to act for a further end; it is an end in itself. Like happiness, which is also an essential candidate for the ultimate end, morality does not appear to be justified in terms of further ends. It is good in itself. Keeping a promise need not be aimed at any further good, such as making everyone happy or making the promise keeper feel good. It is enough, or at least it seems to be, that one has done what is right. That is, one has satisfied an end in itself, whatever other considerations may also be present to complicate one's fidelity.

One thing that "being reasonable" does *not* mean is this: it is not the inhuman ideal of being without passion, detached, and aloof. We sometimes say, "Be reasonable," as a contrast to "Don't be emotional." But there is nothing in our conception of reason or rationality that commands a life without love or, for that matter, without anger or pride or indignation. In fact, our emotions may themselves be perfectly reasonable (as well as unreasonable) and may also be an essential ingredient in forming the attachments, as in love and friendship, which make up the good life. To be rational, on this account, is always to keep intrinsic goods in mind, including not only happiness and morals, but also that sort of involvement without which we are, at best, disinterested spectators in life.

THREE

ELEMENTS OF
THE ETHICAL LIFE

INTRINSIC GOODS: HAPPINESS, KNOWLEDGE, AND THE MEANING OF INTEGRITY

The good life, Aristotle tells us, can be summarized in the word "happiness." Happiness is an intrinsic good, an end in itself, if anything is; indeed, Aristotle tells us that the very word "happiness" (*eudaimonia*) is nothing but the name of the ultimate good in life, its highest end, the *summum bonum* toward which all our activities and our hopes are aimed.

And yet, happiness is not the only candidate for that high honor. We have also seen that morality is often described as a "trump" set of principles, as an end in itself, as a highest good that requires no further end (no nonmoral reasons) for its justification. There are other candidates for the status of intrinsic goods: pleasure and knowledge, for example, and also love and friendship. But what if these intrinsic goods collide and contradict one another? What if morality and happiness sometimes stand opposed? What if love sometimes makes happiness impossible, contrary to our romantic "all you need is love" fantasies? (However deeply in love they may have been, Romeo and Juliet were certainly not *eudaimon*.)

Knowledge has always been a particularly attractive and troublesome candidate for being an end in itself, an intrinsic good that needs no further end or justification. Plato and Aristotle clearly identify knowledge with the pursuit of happiness, for example. Both authors insist that one can't be happy without being knowledgeable and that, being knowledgable, one will not and cannot do wrong. (All bad action, in other words, is the result of ignorance of some kind.) Aristotle further argues that the best life, the life that is even "closest to the gods," is the life of contemplation, the thoughtful life, in which knowledge is our highest goal and learning our constant activity.

Even if we disagree with Plato and Aristotle about the impossibility of knowing the good and doing wrong or about the exclusive superiority of the contemplative life, it is hard to disagree with them about the basic idea that knowledge and reflection (contemplation) are important to ethics and the good life. One need not take the strict Kantian line that morality consists of principles of practical reason in order to recognize that knowing what one is doing is essential to good living. Only so much of our activity can be unreflective, unconscious, or habitual. Many of the activities we prize most in ourselves are deeply involved in knowledge and intelligence, whether we are engaging in the purely practical activity of engineering a bridge or a building or the heroic moral activity of standing up and arguing for a moral principle. (Supporting a moral principle is not an activity unique to Socrates; many lawyers, politicians, and businesspeople do it every day.) Ethics cannot consist of merely doing what we do; it also includes the reasons for our doing what we do and our knowledge of ends and consequences and the sense that what we are doing is right. Indeed, both Kant and Aristotle argue with remarkable similarity that the ultimate end of human life must be rational activity, since mere "animal" happiness could be better assured by natural instinct and unthinking behavior. Knowledge does not necessarily make us happy. (Oedipus would have been much happier had he never found out that he had married his mother and murdered his father.) But knowledge does make us human, and that alone has been sufficient for many philosophers to call it an end in itself.

There are problems, however, with the notion that knowledge is an end in itself. First of all, there is the danger that the search for knowledge will eclipse other aspects of the good life, such as love and friendship, community involvement, and perhaps even morality. Candid interviews with Nobel Prize–winning scientists sometimes show that people will occasionally "stop at nothing" to get knowledge; indeed, it is such single-mindedness and even ruthlessness that makes possible some of the greatest breakthroughs in knowledge. Second, this same single-mindedness makes possible that mad-scientist figure, exemplified in literature by Doctor Frankenstein, who often proclaims the good of knowledge above any other concerns or dangers. Third, even without such villainous characters, science has recently proved to be dangerous indeed; the scientists who created the atomic bomb were motivated by the best intentions of knowledge and patriotism, but the dangers of their discoveries, as well as the advantages and virtues, are undeniable. Fourth, the very meaning of "knowledge" is not at all clear. We have thus far assumed that knowledge consists in knowing what one is doing and the search for scientific truth. But what about that sense of knowledge that is concerned with religious faith rather than with action and science? "The truth shall make you free," in the Bible, does not refer to the wonders of science, no matter how many secular college campuses have the statement carved on their buildings. Does knowledge have to be defined by the scientific method, or are there other concerns which are equally or more important in its definition? Such questions and considerations show us that even if our respect for knowledge is in some sense unquestioned, the nature of knowledge and its role in the good life is complicated. It will not do to say simply that knowledge is an end in itself and independent of all other considerations; it is an essential ingredient in the good life, but it is not (for most people) an intrinsic good which is not to be questioned or limited by anything else.

The same might be argued about love and friendship. We often praise love absurdly, as if it alone can provide everything in life. Yet, it is obvious that love alone is not enough and, in fact, sometimes can be downright disastrous. Even morality has its limits. We do not admire a person who insists on keeping even the pettiest promise to the exclusion of all other concern for circumstances or the well-being of others. (The great Czech author Franz Kafka made his best friend promise to burn all his manuscripts; luckily for us, the friend broke the promise for the greater good of everyone.) Pleasure too has its limits. We can all think of pleasures which, however intense, are nevertheless disgusting or intolerably dangerous. But this is to say that, perhaps apart from happiness, all our intrinsic goods are in fact not that at all. In general, they are desirable and valuable enough so that their importance is unquestioned. But they are nevertheless an intrinsic part of the good life, which means that their value must always be balanced against the other ingredients of the good life.

Much of ethics and ethical living, accordingly, is the attempt to *synthesize* these ends and to make them work together. Indeed, one of the continuing efforts of the great moral philosophers, from Aristotle in ancient times to Kant and most modern moralists, has always been to develop a viewpoint within which these various elements fit together in a coherent and livable way. The much-discussed opposition of selfish pleasures and morality is a particularly crude example of the conflict of ends, but even in the more honorable cases of prudence versus morality, our well-being in life depends upon our ability to sort out right from wrong, to see through such conflicts to the course of action to be pursued. For Plato and Aristotle, happiness and the good life consist of freedom from conflict, "the harmony of one's soul" as well as the integration of one's desires and virtue and the well-being of the entire community. Thus, we might say that the key to happiness and the good life is *integrity,* which means not only honor and honesty but also wholeness, completeness, "oneness." (An "integer" in mathematics is a whole number.)

Is happiness an end in itself? A great many ethicists have said so, and there is at least one sense in which happiness is the definitive end of the good life. That sense is Aristotle's (which he shared with other Greeks) according to which "happiness" (as *eudaimonia*) is by definition the name of the good life, whatever other goals might enter into its composition. The word simply means the goal of the good life. Happiness, however, designates two very different features of the good life, which we might distinguish as *feeling* happy and as *flourishing* (or "doing well," a more literal translation of *eudaimonia*). One might feel happy even if trapped in a miserable life filled with failure and misfortune. But to say that one is happy in the sense of flourishing is to say that life itself is also going well, that one is in fact succeeding in most of one's goals and leading a full and fortunate life. It is worth noting that Aristotle would not have recognized the first sense of happiness at all. We, on the other hand, seem to give feeling happy our top priority, especially in times of failure or misfortune. Indeed, we are often told, the truly happy person is one who can be happy even in the worst of times. Aristotle would not have even understood what we were talking about. Happiness requires a satisfying, integrated life, not just the feeling of contentment.

As a feeling, happiness is often taken to be a general kind of pleasure. [John Stuart Mill conflates the two, as we see again in the following section, "Pleasure (and Pain)".] When happiness connotes flourishing, however, it is often defined as the satisfaction of all (or at least most of) our desires. Of course, it would be absurd to say that a person is flourishing if virtually all his or her desires are frustrated and all ambitions had ended in failure. But there are at least three reasons to qualify the apparently plausible view that happiness (as flourishing) is the satisfaction of our desires. The first is that many of our desires and much of our happiness are, in an important sense, not just "ours" at all. For example, someone's life and happiness may be bound up in the well-being of one's family, or the success of one's business firm, or the thriving of the community. These goals may still be the object of one's desires, but it would be misleading to suggest that happiness is just the satisfaction of one's own desires; it may be the satisfaction of other people's desires and other standards and goals as well. Indeed, this fact led Aristotle to suggest that a person's happiness continues after he or she is dead, for the goals and standards desired in life—for example, the success and happiness of one's children—continue after one's life is over. (Of course, this concept would make no sense at all in the feeling view of happiness.)

The second reason for hesitating to accept the view that happiness is the satisfaction of desires is the insatiability of some of the most important desires in life; they are never satisfied. Artists and writers are rarely satisfied once and for all; each work is a step to the next. (Thus, one sees the tragedy of young artists and writers who do their best work when they are very young, and spend the rest of their lives in that most unhappy state of "going downhill.") Very religious people often insist that faith is more quest than conquest; perfect faith, while an ideal to be striven for all one's life, is never actually attainable. Even pleasure may be important not so much in its enjoyment as in its pursuit;

the great German poet Goethe has his lecherous character Faust exclaim, "From desire I rush to satisfaction, but from satisfaction I leap to desire." Happiness, in other words, need not be the product of our efforts but may be those efforts themselves. Or, as a French wit once put it, "Love desires not satisfaction but prolongation." So, too, it may be with life and happiness—not satisfaction but lifelong effort and continuing passion are what count.

The third reason for not thinking of happiness as the satisfaction of our desires consists of other considerations we discussed in "The Limits of Satisfaction" section in Part Two. There is an all-important difference between the satisfaction of our desires and the satisfaction of our *selves,* even if it goes without saying that self-satisfaction includes the satisfaction of our goals and ambitions as well. It is this overall self-satisfaction, which incorporates within it our concern for the well-being of others and the ethos of our community, that is the ultimate meaning of integrity—a whole life rather than conflicting fragments of satisfied desires.

PLEASURE (AND PAIN)

One of the candidates for an end in itself, in fact often the most popular one, is pleasure. At the opposite side of the pleasure scale stands the most plausible candidate for what is most to be avoided—pain. Of course, we have to distinguish between momentary and immediate pleasures and pains and those of longer duration and those yet to come. Most people are willing to suffer some momentary pain (e.g., at the dentist) in order to avoid a much longer term pain later on, and most people will forgo an immediate pleasure if some greater pleasure lies on the horizon or if some excruciating pain awaits them as a penalty. We might say that pleasure is an end in itself and pain is to be avoided in itself, but this is not to say that all pleasures are equally desirable or that all pains are equally to be avoided. Nor is it to assume that pleasure is the only end in itself, or pain the only thing to be avoided as such. "Because I enjoy it" and "Because it hurts" may be adequate most of the time in accounting for our actions, but there will always be other considerations (morality, taste, self-respect) which may make a pleasure unacceptable or a pain necessary.

Hedonism is the view that pleasure is the sole end of human activity and the key to the good life (coupled with the avoidance of pain). Like egoism (with which it is often conflated), hedonism admits of two distinct interpretations, a *psychological* version which insists that all our actions are in fact aimed at attaining pleasure and avoiding pain, and an *ethical* version which says that all our actions *ought* to be aimed at pleasure and the avoidance of pain. The first thesis is often used as the basis of the second, on the ground that if all our actions are hedonistic anyway, certainly it makes no sense to insist that we ought to act otherwise. Less reduntantly, many hedonists readily admit that not all our actions are hedonistic; indeed, the importance of hedonism turns on the observation that many people seem to feel guilty about their pleasures and cause themselves much unnecessary pain.

It is often suggested (by psychological hedonists) that all human activity is motivated by the pursuit of pleasure and the avoidance of pain. In an obvious sense, it is true that we do avoid pain and we do try to do those things that are most enjoyable. Moreover, we are often pained (mentally if not physically) when we do things that we don't want to do, and we typically feel pleasure when we do what we want to do. Nevertheless, we also do much that is painful, including the cramp-producing exercises we do to "get into shape" or the boredom-inducing visits to grandmother which have become obligatory. Is it so obvious that we always do some things in order to avoid some greater pain or to produce some offsetting pleasure? Furthermore, the meaning of the "pursuit of pleasure" is not altogether clear. Lusting for a piece of cheesecake in the store window, then rushing in to buy it, would certainly be an example; so, perhaps, would saving up the money to buy a small sailboat. But what about a person who enjoys reading theology or playing a good, hard game of tennis? Are such activities the "pursuit of pleasure," or would it be much more accurate to say that the pleasure in some sense "accompanies" the activities pursued? It is generally agreed that pleasure has some role in happiness and the good life, but the exact nature of that role is not at all clear.

Aristotle puts happiness at the top of his ethics, as the highest goal, the *summum bonum*. He does not, however, give similar status to pleasure. Indeed, twice in his *Ethics* he considers in detail the various claims of the hedonists of his own times, and he rejects them. Pleasure is not an end, he argues; it is rather the *complement* of good actions. In other words, we do not do something good because we enjoy it so much as we enjoy ourselves because we are doing something good. One does not play basketball in order to get pleasure but, rather one gets pleasure from playing basketball because it is something that one wants to do. (This may be true even if one's playing is poor.) Hedonism is false, then, because pleasure is not the goal of our actions. We get pleasure because we attain the goals of our actions, but this means that the achievement of those goals, not the enjoyment of accomplishing them, constitutes happiness. The good life will include pleasure and enjoyment, therefore, but that does not mean that pleasure itself is the end or the main ingredient in the good life.

Pleasure is defended as the highest good of John Stuart Mill's "utilitarianism." Indeed, Mill claims that everything that we do—whatever other reasons we might provide—is aimed at pleasure and the avoidance of pain, which he calls "happiness." It is here that Mill differs most from Aristotle, who emphatically denies that what he calls "happiness" (*eudaimonia*) is to be identified with pleasure. Mill's harsh rebuttal of those who try to make utilitarianism sound vulgar or voluptuous because of its emphasis on pleasure reflects the disapproval of hedonism throughout the history of ethics. Indeed, the heart of Mill's theory is his attempt to make the notion of "pleasure" more respectable.

It is with this in mind that he introduces his novel theory of the "quality" of pleasure. Mill's mentor, Jeremy Bentham, had developed an earlier version of utilitarianism in which happiness and the good life were to be calculated on the basis of sheer *quantity* of pleasure. His "principle of utility" insists, quite simply, that one always ought to do that action which will bring the greatest good (that is, the greatest pleasure, the least pain) to the greatest number of people. An act is good insofar as it is "useful" in this sense, that is, insofar as it maximizes pleasure and minimizes pain.

Mill accepts this principle of utility as the basis of his ethics too, but it is worth noting how negligible a role "utility" plays in his discussion. He does not suggest that some pleasures are more "useful" than others; in fact, the utility of pleasure seems not to be at all in question, particularly since the "higher" pleasures typically consist of such activities as reading and thinking and enjoying the arts, which may be laudable but hardly useful. By contrast, Mill hardly mentions the pleasures of physical work and economic production, although he was, we might add, one of the leading economists of the nineteenth century. He seems to have viewed physical labor as relentless drudgery, without pleasure of any kind (much more firmly than did Marx, who was in London about the same time).

There can be no mistaking what Mill means by "higher" pleasures; they are those enjoyments which are more intellectual, artistic, or spiritual (although Mill was basically an atheist) as opposed to those which are more physical and physiological. The pleasures of good food, sex, and other physical activities are not excluded, but they are given a distinctively lower value on Mill's "quality" scale of pleasures. He does not exclude or ignore noble actions as sources of pleasure, but he clearly suggests that nobility and intellect go hand in hand, and that "men lose their high aspirations as they lose their intellectual tastes." It is Socrates who supplies Mill with his most prominent example of the "higher" pleasures, however dissatisfied the great philosopher may have been with his own intellectual accomplishments. It is a pig that provides the paradigm of enjoyment of the "lower" pleasures, thus setting up the scale in the most biased possible way. But are all pleasures of the intellect so noble? And must we consider all physical pleasures as piglike? Is enjoying an excellent bottle of Bordeaux really on a par with wallowing in the mud? And are the joys of abstruse metaphysics necessarily "higher" (that is, better) than the simple physical pleasure of giving or receiving an effective back-rub?

The real problem with Mill's conception of the "quality" of pleasures is not the bias of his scale in favor of the intellectual and against the physical, however. We can still readily agree to some distinction between the qualities of pleasures. For example, we would agree that the pleasure one gets from having cooked and served a good dinner to one's friends is much better than the pleasures of a sadist, even if the sadist should get more enjoyment out of his or her perversions. And isn't there something debatably "better" about enjoying a

Mozart opera rather than picking one's toes in Poughkeepsie? But it is Mill's *criterion* for distinguishing the qualities of pleasures that is dubious; he says that the former pleasure is preferred to the latter by all, or most, competent judges who have experienced both kinds of pleasure. But is it so clear that we would, or do, choose the higher pleasures even if we have experienced them? And what do we mean by "choose," here? Public television often programs Shakespeare or Beethoven opposite a network series of undeniable worthlessness, and a vast audience of those who have experienced both types of program choose to watch the worthlessness. What does this mean? If questioned, surely most people who have read, seen, and appreciated Shakespeare will *say* that they prefer the "higher" pleasure of Shakespeare. What they *do,* however, is watch "Mork and Mindy" or "Kojak." Which counts as a choice? And how does either succeed as a plausible test of quality? Indeed, isn't the (indisputable) difference in quality assumed beforehand? And don't people choose in part because of that difference? The sad fact seems to be that most people choose on the basis of the quantity of simple pleasure, but the philosophic point is that the choice—on whatever grounds—is not the test of quality; if anything, quality survives despite the majority choices.

What Mill has tried to do is to reduce the vulgarity and "voluptuousness" of Bentham's quantitative pleasure model of ethics and replace it with a two-dimensional model of both quantity and quality. But the beauty of Bentham's ethics is that it reduces all ethical calculations to a single dimension, and this is just what Mill has undone. How will we tell when one pleasure is of a greater quality than another? How can we decide whether quality overrides quantity, or vice versa? (When is an extravagant physical pleasure more desirable than a modest intellectual or artistic pleasure? When is a good philosophy lecture worth more than a day at the beach?) And since "utility" is not even mentioned as a criterion, and would be implausible as a defense of most of Mill's preferred "higher" pleasures anyway, have we not moved back to square 1, and opened up—rather than solved—the question of the *summum bonum* all over again?

SELF

At the heart of ethics is the self, the responsible (or irresponsible) individual who acts, the person who suffers or enjoys the fruits of his or her activity, the character that develops and is displayed through a lifetime of behavior (remember that the word "ethics" is derived from the concept of "character" [ethos]). The German philosopher Nietzsche, while he has certain reservations about the reality of the self, nevertheless insists throughout his works that the most important factor in ethics is not morality or social rules and customs or even happiness but, rather, the value of the self, the worth of the person in question, that person's character, virtues, and abilities. But, as Nietzsche himself recognizes, the notion of self is not a simple one; there is no "thing" inside of us which is the self. Indeed, as David Hume and Sartre also argue, when one actually looks "inside" ("introspects") to find one's true self, one finds nothing at all.

Such doubts about the self have always pervaded philosophy. Plato was not satisfied with the biological conception of ourselves as constantly changing organisms of flesh and blood, and so he defended the notion of an immortal soul, distinct from, and infinitely more durable than, the body. Christianity too developed this notion of an intangible, eternal soul "within" us, and for many people, this intangible self became more real than the flesh and blood self of everyday life. René Descartes famously planted the self at the center of philosophy with his much-repeated and often parodied "I think, therefore I am," but he too then found great difficulty in explaining the connection between this conscious mental self and the physical body to which it seems so intimately attached. David Hume, as we noted previously, doubted that there is any such a thing as a self (even though he too developed an ethics of character instead of a morality of rational rules). In reaction to Hume, Immanuel Kant defended the notion of the ethical self as the *real* self, essentially free, rational, and responsible for our actions and our moral worth. For some of the philosophers following Kant (for example, the German idealist G. W. F. Hegel), the active self becomes literally everything. For other philosophers, it is virtually nothing. Between those two extremes lies the ethical world, in which the nature and value of the self are in constant dispute.

We talk about ourselves (that is, our selves) as if each of us were obviously a single, unified, coherent self, or, if there are different parts of the self, as if they play together in perfect harmony like the instruments of a good symphony orchestra. (Indeed, this musical analogy in terms of harmony was often used by the Greeks to characterize the well-functioning self, and it has been similarly employed ever since.) But, with a little investigation, it soon becomes clear that what we call "self" has several very different aspects; which of them are essential to the self and its worth is the focus of one of the longest-running disputes in not only philosophy but religion and psychology as well.

Self as Agent

In ethics, the most important sense of self is of self as *agent,* the doer of deeds, the hero as well as the perpetrator of crimes. The self as agent is to be distinguished, for example, from the self as detached *knower,* say in science, in much the same way that the players in a football game must be distinguished from the fans who are watching. The agents are responsible for the action; the observers merely take note of what they do. The actions of agents must also be distinguished from the mere events and happenings that befall inanimate (that is, nonagent) objects. A leaf may fall from a tree, but it does not decide to do so, or try to do so, or succeed in doing so at will. People as agents, on the other hand, decide to do what they will do, try to do what they want to do, and succeed or fail accordingly. (Of course, a person who falls out of an airplane is much like the leaf—but then, once out of the plane he or she is no longer an agent in the critical sense.)

The self as agent is the initiator of actions. It is not, like a wheel in a mechanism, merely one more link in a causal process. Even in a mechanical cooperative venture, such as passing memos around the office or notes across the classroom, each individual must agree to participate and decide to accept and pass on the paper in question, and each person can, if wanting to, decide to thwart the process by tearing up the paper, by writing a nasty note on top of it, by passing it back in the direction from whence it came instead of passing it on. To be an agent is to have this power of refusal, to be capable of being obstinate, difficult, or perverse as well as cooperative and helpful. To be an agent is to take matters into one's own hands, to have control over the situation, and to be responsible as well.

Some philosophers, notably Immanuel Kant, discuss the self as agent in terms of what they call *will*. In the beginning of his ethics, for instance, Kant insists that "nothing is good without qualification . . . except a *good will*." Part of what he means is that it is the person as pure agent who is the essential focus of ethics. That initial act of mind, that "push" that we sometimes give to ourselves when we decide to act, is what ethics is all about. Following that little push (sometimes called a "volition" or an "act of will"), there is the action itself and the *consequences* of that action. And because we are responsible as agents for that initial mental push which gets everything going, we would probably insist that we are responsible as well for the action and the consequences. This is a matter of some contention in ethics, however, since some philosophers (Kant, among others) want to emphasize our responsibility for the initial willing but deemphasize what follows, while other ethicists (John Stuart Mill, for example) emphasize the nature of the consequences and deemphasize the act of will. In any case, however, it is the *doing* that counts, the fact that we act as agents rather than simply react as objects without a mind or a will of our own.

Self as Rational

Along with the conception of self as agent often goes the view of the self as essentially rational. Kant, for example, talks of the active self as "rational will" and insists that one of the outstanding characteristics of our selves as agents is the fact that we not only initiate actions, but that we also plan and initiate actions according to rational principles—that is, according to the rules of morality. Indeed, for Kant, ethics is precisely the business of "practical reason," and the self of ethics is accordingly defined in terms of its rationality. Aristotle, too, defines human beings as "rational animals" and so also insists that our selves as agents in ethics must be understood as rational, as capable of abstract thought and planning, rather than as mere creatures of habit and impulse, like most of the "lower" animals.

Self as Soul

In a book on theological ethics, the concept of self which would take top priority would be the concept of *soul*. Our "real" self—according to this concept—is quite distinct from the more ordinary aspects of ourselves. Most importantly, it is distinct from—and infinitely outlasts—the physical organism in which it is embodied. One finds such a concept of self, for example, in the Christian ethics of St. Augustine. But one also finds it in non-Christian authors—for example, in Socrates's argument in Plato's *Crito*.

Self as Whole Human Being

The biological category *Homo sapiens,* on the other hand, already tells us that the concept of being human and the concept of being rational (or, literally, "knowing") have long been tied together. The self, accordingly, has often been conceived as an organic whole—the complete human being, nothing less. Plato and Aristotle argued this before Christianity; such thinkers as David Hume and Friedrich Nietzsche have since argued it against the Christian concept of self as soul. But this is not to say that an organic conception of self is *only* biological. The notion of self as essentially human has typically been characterized in terms of our most dramatic difference from (most of) the animal kingdom. This difference comprises our ability to speak and think and speculate on the nature of life, death, and the cosmos. Indeed, we find in both Kant and Aristotle an argument to the effect that our ethics must be bound to reason just because only we, in the animal world, have that capacity; it is unique with us, and why would we have it if we were not supposed to use it? (Both Kant and Aristotle maintain that reason has a *purpose,* Kant because he believes that we were created by a wise God, Aristotle because he believes that the whole universe—and everything in it—has a purpose.) To see the self as a human being, however, is also to break down the sense of self as an isolated individual and insist (as both Kant and Aristotle do) that we must see ourselves always as part of a larger whole, as part of "humanity" (though "humanity," for Aristotle, was limited to the Greeks) with moral obligations to every other human being.

Self as Sentient

Hedonism, in particular, is bound to a sense of self that is not essentially an agent, not essentially rational, which may or may not be human. It is the self as the locus of the feelings of pleasure and pain. Of course, no one would deny that we do have pleasures and suffer pains, but it is something quite different to elevate this sentient self to the status of a "real" or "highest" self. Aristotle, for example, would readily admit that we, like most animals, are moved by pleasures and pains, but he would insist that this is one of the "lower aspects" of the self, if indeed it deserves to be mentioned as part of the self at all. But at this point, we start to see something of tremendous ethical importance about the concept of "self" in ethics; it is itself an ethical term, which all of us use to praise or diminish one aspect of ourselves or of others. One philosopher insists that the "true" self is the rational self; another argues that the "real" self is the self of feelings and desires; still another maintains that the "soul," the metaphysically real self, is only that which is tied to, and yearns for, God and the infinite. The choice of a concept of self is already one of the definitive moves in ethics.

Self as Character

We have not yet mentioned what many philosophers and most other people sometimes consider the most obvious sense of self-- oneself as an individual, as a particular person with individual (though not necessarily unique) character- istics. What makes me myself, one might say, is my own peculiar sense of humor, the way I respond to my friends, my special abilities and personality quirks. Indeed, one sense of self that has always been of particular importance in ethics is precisely that sense of *character,* so praised by Aristotle and Hume, in which the virtues are well manifested. But character in this sense is not just "being a character" in the sense of being odd or eccentric, and it means some- thing more than simply having individual characteristics, which, of course, we all have. Character in this special sense refers to a person who has moral vir- tues, who is courageous, generous, temperate, and honorable, whatever that may mean in a particular society. (There is honor, we are told, even among thieves.)

These aspects of self might be supplemented by several more, but the reader may already have noticed that discussions of self tend to slip into two different perspectives, which we might, with caution, follow tradition in calling "inside" and "outside," respectively. Kant's emphasis on will, the Christian emphasis on the soul, the hedonists' emphasis on feelings, all of these are concerned with the "inner" aspects of a person; indeed, they may not even be visible to anyone else. Theories of self have often focused on such inner aspects; at the end of the seventeenth century, the British philosopher John Locke, for example, pre- sented the view of self that is still most defended by philosophers: The self is essentially a matter of our memories and their unity, and these are to be dis- tinguished from the unity and continuity of our bodies. (Thus, philosophers have speculated ever since on what would happen if we should find ourselves— that is, our minds—relocated in some other body, say in another person, in a dog, or even in a toaster.) But there are also views of the self which emphasize not the "inner" but the "outer," those aspects of us which are knowable by other people, in fact, perhaps better known by them than by us. Other people, for example, may be much better judges of our character than we are ourselves. A person might well be the last to know that he or she is ignorant, generous, or cowardly. Thus, too, some philosophers (Aristotle, most notably) have defined the self as a strictly *social* self; what goes on in people's minds is not nearly so important as the way they each fit into society and play the roles which make them useful citizens.

There is one other possibility, however, which we will only mention here. There may be, in a profound sense, *no* self as such, not in the sense that Hume couldn't find one when he looked, but in the sense that the self is something we *create* through our actions. This is the position of the existentialist Jean-Paul Sartre; indeed, he makes it the defining thesis of his philosophy. "Man makes himself," he says. He means that self is found neither "inside" as soul or will or feelings nor "outside" as a character already formed by our heredity and upbringing. In his view, we are rather the characters that we create by proving ourselves in the world.

FREEDOM AND RESPONSIBILITY

There would be little point to doing ethics if we did not believe that we are all to some extent *free* to choose one goal rather than another, to act one way rather than another way. To say that a person is an agent is to insist that not only does that person have a causal role in a situation, but also that he or she is more than one of the causes of an event taking place. The force of gravity or the action of the wind can be a cause in that sense. An agent must be free and responsible, free to choose whether to carry out an action, and responsible for it and its consequences after carrying it out. (One may be responsible for *not* carrying out an action, and the consequences of not doing so as well.)

It is one of the presuppositions of morality that we are free beings who can make decisions and act voluntarily. We are not machines or robots who do only what we are programmed to do. Thus, Aristotle includes in his ethical treatise an analysis of what it is for an action to be "voluntary" (it must not be externally compelled, and it must not be out of ignorance, he says). Kant calls freedom "a postulate of practical reason," meaning that there can be no reason—no morality—without it. But not only is freedom the presupposition of most ethical theories; some philosophers have elevated it to the highest value in ethics as well. Jean-Paul Sartre, most notably, takes freedom to be the goal as well as the basis of human consciousness. Ethics, according to Sartre, is the realization of our freedom through action.

Hand in hand with freedom goes responsibility. Responsibility means, first of all, effectively bringing something about, whether or not one intended to do so. The drunken driver is responsible for having hit the dog, even if he did so out of incompetence in driving and ignorance that the dog was there. Second, responsibility—in a more morally significant sense—includes an assumption of freedom. The driver was responsible, in part, because he was free to choose whether to drive or not to drive, to drink or not to drink, to take this road or another one, to drive faster or slower, to watch more carefully or drive as recklessly as he did. (One might say that a computer is responsible for a certain result, but only in the causal sense. Leaving aside certain science fiction fantasies ["Hal" in Arthur Clarke's *2001*], the computer has no choice in its production of results and is therefore not responsible.) Finally, in ethics, responsibility has a distinctively moral sense over and above the supposition of freedom; this is the sense in which one is responsible for doing—or not doing—what one *ought* to do.

It is one thing to say that a person *caused* an event; it is something else to say that that person had a choice and was *free* to do or not do it; it is something else again to say that what the person did carried a *moral* responsibility, that is, it was governed by considerations of right and wrong. A person who walks into a flying pie and prevents it from hitting its intended target is responsible in the first sense. A person who chooses to bake an apple instead of an apricot pie is responsible in the second sense. But a builder who chooses to scrimp and cheat on a construction, which later falls down and kills eight people, is responsible in the third sense as well. The concepts of *praise* and *blame,* accordingly, are essential moral concepts having to do with responsibility. They designate responsibility (who did it, who chose to do it); at the same time, they make a moral judgment of right or wrong, good or bad (one is blamed for wrong or bad acts; one is praised for right or good acts.)

Freedom in some sense is necessary to our concept of responsibility; the fact that a person "could have done otherwise" seems essential to our attributions of praise and blame. A difficult question arises, however, when we consider freedom itself as a value, as an end to be desired and fought for. It is one thing to say that because people are free, they are responsible for their actions. It is something quite different to say that it is a good thing that they are free. It seems from what we say that we take freedom to be the ultimate good, an end in itself, more precious than even life itself. ("Give me liberty, or give me death," proclaimed an early American patriot.) Why is this so?

Freedom is, first of all, freedom from unreasonable restraints. Being forbidden by the authorities to travel or spend money as we like seems to most Americans as an unreasonable restraint. Having to obey the law of gravity is not an unreasonable restraint, and so this is not considered a fetter on our freedom. (In a recent Monty Python movie, one of the male characters protests the fact that he is not allowed to have babies; his comrades unconvincingly comfort him with the assurance that he has the *right* to have babies.) Being thrown in jail is an obvious curtailment of freedom; putting oneself through medical school—

though the hours and the food might be equally bad—is not. Freedom, in other words, is first of all a sense of ourselves as agents, as having a *choice* in what we do. Our great respect for freedom resides primarily in our sense that we *ought* to be allowed to do what we want to do, subject to *reasonable* restraints. (One should not be allowed to yell "fire" in a crowded auditorium, for example.) But, in the ethical terms "ought" and "reasonable," we see that the concept of freedom is itself a morally loaded concept; to say what counts as freedom in particular cases is part of, not prior to, ethics. Deciding what counts as an "unreasonable restraint" is one of the central questions in social and political ethics.

The very word "freedom" is a battlecry, filled with excitement. It is clear that we are now concerned with a political concept, more substantial than mere freedom as the abstract ability "to have done otherwise." When the concept of freedom is under discussion, accordingly, it is typically conflated with many other goods and opposed to any number of evils which may have nothing to do with it. For example, freedom is often contrasted with slavery, and the picture that comes to mind is a portrait of inhuman horror—of beaten, shackled, broken souls forced to do the most menial and exhausting labor with, at most, mere subsistence as their reward. But, of course, lack of freedom in our sense need not mean slavery, and our revulsion against many of the worst features of that bondage has nothing to do with freedom. Consider, for instance, the inhabitants of a happy little village somewhere in the world: food is plentiful, there is no threat of war, and there is little violence. Everyone is born into a role in the village and knows from childhood what he or she must do and will do. Life is more than sufficiently full to make sure that people aren't bored, and there is more than enough of everything, including tribal honors and neighborly love for everyone. The necessary condition of this happy state, however, is that people are not only restrained from doing other than what is expected of them (the penalty for even slight eccentricity is exile or death); they are brought up in such a way that they are not even allowed to be aware of the alternatives. (There are, therefore, no imported books or movies.) But because everyone has been brought up not only to accept but to enjoy this life, the desire to do anything different is extremely rare—and so the actual imposition of restraints and penalties is also rare, in fact almost a matter of myth rather than history. There is no freedom (there is not even a word for it) but there is no unhappiness either.

Now is it so clear that these people would be better off if they were given our valuable notion of freedom? Perhaps *we* might say (as in so many "Star Trek" episodes) that "freedom is what makes us human." But rest assured that a spokesperson for the happy village would find our concept of "human" perverse in the extreme, a kind of voluntary chaos and a guarantee of *un*happiness. "How can people know who they are and be assured of well-being," we can imagine the spokesperson saying, "if people are 'free' to do whatever they want.

We determine, as well as provide, what they want, and that way everyone is satisfied. It is with choice that there comes to be unhappiness and confusion. It is happiness that is important—not your "freedom".

What this little fable shows is not that freedom is not valuable, but that, to the extent that we are attracted to the comfort and security of this little village, it is not the *only* thing that we value. In short, we must not automatically assume that the good life comes only with freedom and is totally unthinkable without it. Of course, given the value we place on individual initiative and the importance of personal desires, no matter how unusual or eccentric, it is essential to our ethics that freedom from unreasonable restraint will be of the highest priority, the key to our sense of self as well as a primary goal of our ethics. It is in this sense that we agree that freedom is worth fighting for—even dying for, but not as a mere abstraction, a word that has too often provided the slogan for battles which have nothing to do with unreasonable restraints. Freedom is worth fighting for because our sense of self depends upon it—and with that, the whole of our ethos and our ethics, including, not least, our profound sense of personal responsibility for what we make of ourselves.

We have characterized freedom, first of all, as freedom from unreasonable restraints. But many philosophers would insist that this is, at best, half a proper definition of "freedom," and a negative one at that. For, in addition to this "freedom from" or *negative freedom,* there is also "freedom to" or *positive freedom.* What good is freedom from restraint, such philosophers as G. W. F. Hegel have asked, if there is nothing for us to do with that freedom, no community to be part of, no institutions in which to participate, nothing worthwhile to be done except satisfy our own short-term needs and pleasures? Thus they suggest that, in addition to freedom from government restrictions and impositions, freedom also requires the provision of a meaningful context for action. In the purely negative sense, we might say that a man who has been fired from his job is "free," but we will not think much of this freedom if he has no alternatives, no way to support himself, and nothing to do.

We can talk about freedom, therefore, in at least three important ways in ethics: (1) as the precondition of responsibility, praise, and blame ("could have done otherwise"); (2) as freedom from unreasonable restraint (with the emphasis on "unreasonable"); and (3) as freedom to participate in meaningful activities and institutions. We can imagine an ethos and an ethics in which one or two of these factors would be all but irrelevant and a third simply taken for granted, but in our ethos and ethics, all three are of the greatest importance; indeed, we cannot imagine our lives without any of them.

THE "FREE WILL" PROBLEM

There is a general problem regarding freedom that has worried philosophers for thousands of years. It is usually called the "free will" problem, and it raises the question of whether anyone is *ever* free. If no one is free, however, it is doubtful that anyone can be properly held responsible and praised or blamed for any action. The problem was stated in a powerful way many years ago by Saint Augustine in a religious context; If God knowingly created us as "fallible" creatures, then how can He hold us responsible for our sins? Why did he not create us as automatically perfect moral beings? In other words, if it was already preordained that we would sometimes act immorally, what sense does it make to blame us for doing so?

The contemporary versions of the problem typically depend on science rather than religion, and in particular, they depend on the scientific thesis that is usually known as *determinism*. (The topic therefore is often called "free will and determinism.") Determinism is the doctrine that every event, including every human action and decision, is caused by other events, which are in turn caused by other events, and so on. There is no supernatural intervention. There is no room for chance, strictly speaking. A coin comes up heads or tails "by chance," but that is only because we are ignorant of the complex and minute factors—twirl of the coin, shape of the edges, distribution of weight, texture of the table surface—that fully determine the way it lands. So too, it is argued, we think that people freely make decisions, that is, decisions that are free from any prior causal determination. But we think this only because we are woefully ignorant of the millions of causes (people's heredity and upbringing, the state of their brains, what they had for breakfast, the last thing a friend said to them before class, the phase of the moon) that similarly determine their every action. In other words, if determinism is true, then freedom is an illusion. And if freedom is an illusion, responsibility is an illusion too.

This very abstract argument has its extremely practical and particular examples. A man has a long history of crimes behind him, and now he is accused of yet another, even more serious and brutal crime. In court, his attorney tearfully tells the jury of a lifetime of bad breaks and abuse, concluding that "this man is not responsible for his crimes; *society* caused him to do this!" In another much-celebrated trial, the young, unbalanced murderer is said to be "not guilty by reason of insanity." In other words, his criminal behavior has been determined by forces beyond his control. Here too we see the problem of "free will and determinism"; if an action is determined by outside forces, the person is not free and not responsible.

The question soon becomes, Are *any* of us *ever* responsible for our actions, no matter how sane, thoughtful, and deliberative we are? It is a matter of some curiosity but not surprising that most of us are more willing to take responsibility for praiseworthy actions than for blameworthy behavior. Where blame is involved, we are all rather ready with our excuses, "mitigating circumstances" which count as determinants of our behavior beyond our control. But what if there are *always* such determinants? Are we then ever free? Can we be held, and can we hold ourselves, responsible for good acts as well as bad?

The history of philosophy is filled with attempts to resolve these questions. We have already noted that, in ancient times, Aristotle tried to define what would count as a "voluntary" action: (1) It must not be done under external compulsion, and (2) it must not be done out of ignorance. But in our era of psychological sophistication, both these criteria are impossibly complex. Is the young man who became a murderer because of psychological problems "acting under external compulsion"? Is a person who obeys the commands of a criminal who is holding a gun not still "free"? What if you obey the illegal request of an employer who threatens the loss of your job? And ignorance, we know, "is no excuse" when it comes to matters of law, nor are we at all clear any more about what a person knows—or doesn't know—about his or her own behavior. Indeed, as we learn more about psychology and neurology, it begins to look more and more as though people's behavior is determined by factors beyond their control. What does this realization mean about their freedom and responsibility?

Many philosophers have simply rejected the determinist doctrine. Some of them have based their arguments on some of the new theories in physics and insisted that the universe is not deterministic; in that case, determinism ceases to be a problem for freedom. (But then, how do we determine our own actions?) Other philosophers have tried to deny determinism by insisting that there *is* such a thing as freedom in the world and that our wills are the most immediate example of this freedom. In the past several hundred years, however, many philosophers, including David Hume, John Stuart Mill, and the American philosopher William James have tried to get around the deterministic thesis without actually denying its truth. They are sometimes called "soft" determinists (the term is James's) because, unlike the "hard" determinists who refuse to believe in free will, they insist that there is room for freedom and responsibility even within the determinist picture.

One version of soft determinism begins with the point, made previously, that although we might suppose that there are in fact many determining factors for each of our actions, we do not, and probably cannot, know what they all are. Accordingly, in our ignorance, we can and must assume that we are free. To say that we act freely is just to say that we don't know all the causes of our behavior.

This rather weak version of soft determinism is typically coupled or contrasted with a more positive view (in Hume and Mill, for example). This reply to determinism begins by agreeing that our every act is determined; indeed, it might even be added that we could not attribute responsibility if our acts were not determined. But the question is, which of the many possible determinants of our action may in fact be the cause (or causes)? If an act was caused by a malfunction of the brain, we can agree that it was not free and the person not responsible. But suppose the action was caused by that set of factors which we refer to as a person's character, that is, his or her habits, traits, and personality. Those are causes too, and they in turn are caused by other causes (heredity, upbringing, education). But nevertheless, we are perfectly justified in calling an action free if it is determined by a person's character, and we are therefore justified in holding people responsible for their actions too. After all, on what better basis do we hold people responsible than on the sort of person they are and the sort of behavior that we thereby expect of them?

Our final version of soft determinism is really not so "soft," and indeed it is, in one sense, a flat denial of determinism. Even if one accepts determinism in the scientist's sense, a serious paradox arises when one attempts to apply this thesis to oneself. This is not just a matter of ignorance, as in our first suggestion; an incoherence exists in the very idea of knowing all the determinants of our behavior. Or, to put the problem in a different way, our knowledge and our reaction to that knowledge are themselves determinants of our behavior.

Let us take an example: Suppose a seriously overweight woman decides to go on a much-needed diet. The determinants of her behavior are, for the most part, fairly evident—appetite, habits, metabolism, tastes, diet, and nutritional requirements, as well as that more obscure set of determinants that we sometimes summarize as "will power" and "discipline." It is easy to imagine that the dieter in question knows all these factors and thus seems to be in as good a position as anyone else to predict the success of the upcoming diet. In fact, given the failure of the preceding 107 diets attempted over the past two years, anyone would be amply justified in predicting that this diet, like the others, will end in an orgy of beer and chocolate, probably by the middle of next week. But now what happens if the dieter makes such a prediction about herself? This is no prediction; it is now a statement of *intention,* a way of giving up in advance. Indeed, the more the dieter is assured by unsympathetic friends that she will fail to keep to the diet, those reminders and the resultant annoyance become further determinants of her continuing the diet until, perhaps out of sheer obstinacy (a major determinant), she actually succeeds, against all expectations.

This final insistence on our freedom is shared by such temperamentally different philosophers as Immanuel Kant and Jean-Paul Sartre. Kant distinguishes very carefully between aspects of ourselves as knowers and as agents; knowledge is deterministic, but action is wholly based on the postulate of freedom. Knowledge, in other words, presupposes determinism as one of its most basic principles. But action presupposes the absence of determinism and our ability to will freely as its most basic principle. And since determinism and freedom apply to us in entirely different aspects of our lives (knowledge and action, respectively), the question of which one is "true" cannot arise. In acting, we *must* think of ourselves as free; the idea that we are determined, in that context, is simply unintelligible.

VIRTUE AND THE VIRTUES

Ethics is concerned with the whole way of life of an ethos and the moral rules that define it, but it is also concerned with individual *character* and with per-

sonal charms and achievements, whether or not these fall under moral principles. The name traditionally given to such a positive feature in a person is a
virtue. (A negative feature, in these terms, is a *vice.*) But, unfortunately, the
confused history of morals has resulted in a confusing ambiguity for this crucial
term. On the one hand, there is a particular feature of a person's character,
such as honesty, wittiness, generosity, or social charm. On the other hand, there
is that general all-encompassing designation of a person's "virtue" and talk of
"virtue" in general, where the word is used as a synonym for "morality."
(Kant, for example, uses the word "virtue" in this way.) Of course, a person
who has virtues will very likely be virtuous, and a virtuous person will no doubt
have at least some virtues. Nevertheless, the two conceptions are distinct. A
person may have many virtues but, nevertheless, lead a sufficiently wild and
unconventional life (even assuming no *im*morality as such) to prohibit even the
plausibility of that person's being called "virtuous." On the other hand, a person, perhaps out of fear of punishment and general inhibition, may well live a
life that is wholly virtuous in the moral sense, and yet be an utter zero when it
comes to questions of excellence. Some good people may nonetheless be dull
and all but useless.

We have already commented (in Part I) that a very different conception of
ethics (and a very different ethos) results from an emphasis on morality and
an emphasis on character. We have already discussed morality at some length;
it is now time to say something more about character and the virtues. Character, we have already pointed out, relates mainly to realizing one's potential
and cultivating those habits which are most important in a particular society.
Some of these habits may have to do with morality in the narrow sense, but
many do not. A person's sense of humor, for example, is a virtue (and lack of
humor a vice), but we would probably not say that humor is one of a person's
moral characteristics, or that he or she is immoral because of a lack of humor.

What is a virtue? We have already said, at several points, that a virtue is
an excellence; it is a feature about us that is exceptional. It must, of course,
also be exceptionally *good*; an exceptional ability to forge checks or kill cats
with a slingshot is not a virtue. Furthermore, it must be considered good within
one's particular society; being able to fight well with a sword and being "the
fastest gun in the West" are no longer virtues in late twentieth-century America. At most, they might be salable skills in Hollywood. Being a crack computer
programmer would not have been a virtue in the Trojan War and having a
superb sense of humor would not have been a virtue in a medieval Carmelite
monastery. Laziness and chastity are not commonly recognized as virtues in
the fast-living urban cultures of much of America.

Philosophers have often argued that morality is defined in part by its universality, but few ethicists have been tempted to say that about the virtues.
Indeed, the most striking thing about the virtues is how they vary from culture
to culture and through history. We take a sense of humor to be of paramount
importance; it is hard for us to accept the fact that there are many societies in

which our sometimes-raucous laughter is considered both foolish and obnoxious. We, on the other hand, take a dim view of tragedy and overconcern with death, but there are many cultures in which attitudes and behavior toward death are core virtues. (Thus, indignation rose among many American philosophers when a European philosopher, Martin Heidegger, called "Being-toward-Death" the single most important aspect of the human condition.) Attitudes toward food and sex vary enormously from culture to culture, and what counts as vice and perversity in one culture is normal and desirable behavior in another. Even friendliness, which we consider a virtue, varies considerably from culture to culture, for not every society prides itself on being as "open" as we are. Indeed, it is all too common for an American to declare another people "unfriendly" where immediate intimacy with free-spending Yankee tourists is not a virtue but a display of either lack of discrimination or dishonesty.

Some common virtues, such as courage and temperance, turn out to have very different meanings in different societies. Courage in Homer's Greece could be measured by one's stalwart behavior in hand-to-hand combat. We most often mention courage in the context of "courage of one's convictions," which is quite something else. President John F. Kennedy once published a book entitled *Profiles in Courage*; the courage in question was that of politicians who were willing to risk reelection. It is not the same virtue as the courage of Achilles when facing a hundred Trojans in battle. Indeed, one might even be led to wonder whether the two uses of the word "courage" have very much at all in common.

To get a concrete idea of at least one well-developed list of virtues which is different from our own, consider the list which, as you may have anticipated, comes from Aristotle. He canonized for all time the virtues of a very particular Athenian society at a very particular moment in its history. It is important to keep in mind that Aristotle's Athens was no longer the Greece of Homer's *Iliad,* no longer a crude tribe in conflict with other crude tribes, but a "polis"— a free and sophisticated city-state (compared with any other society in ancient history) with a relatively representative government and a rich heritage of art, philosophy, and statesmanship. Courage in battle is still an important virtue— in fact, the first virtue that Aristotle mentions—but it is by no means the only or the most important one. Achilles and Agamemnon, two heroes of the Trojan War, would have been considered barbarians in Aristotle's Athens.

Here is Aristotle's list of virtues:

Courage	Friendliness
Temperance	Truthfulness
Liberality	Wittiness
Magnificence	Shame
Pride	Justice
Good temper	

One virtue missing from the list—we might call it a general virtue which includes virtually all the others—is honor. Indeed, one might well suggest that the summation of the Athenian virtues is just this honor, which includes being held in high public esteem as well as always acting in such a way that public esteem will never be challenged. This is a very different conception of virtue from the warrior virtues of the *Iliad,* and very different again from the piety virtues of a medieval monastic order or the efficiency virtues of a modern-day business manager.

The first thing to notice about this list of virtues is that it clearly includes virtues which we would not consider such: pride, for instance. We think of pride as a vice, or at best as a kind of defensiveness. The closest we come to understanding Aristotle's virtue is in our accusation, "Have you no pride?!" But Aristotle obviously means more than the unwillingness to humiliate oneself. To be proud is to see oneself as superior—because one *is,* after all, superior. And it is to act as if one really were superior as well, an attitude in our society that is deplored in general and despised in particular in politicians and national leaders—just those people who concern Aristotle the most and for whom pride is a most important virtue.

At the same time, we notice that some of our virtues are not on the list. Perhaps most evident, as the opposite of pride, is the virtue of humility. Aristotle's Athenians would not consider this a virtue at all, but rather, a vice, a sign of weakness or insipidness. So, too, notice the absence of at least some cardinal Christian virtues—faith and hope, for example. (Charity is, in a way, included in "liberality," but it is quite different from the Christian virtue.) Indeed, a modern American visitor to ancient Athens would very likely be appalled by the society we have so idealized and idolized for so many centuries.

The names of the virtues are often misleading, not only because of the usual difficulties of translation but also because of the vast difference between the context and culture in which these virtues and their names took part and our own. "Temperance," for example, is not at all the abstinence that we refer to by that name; indeed, Aristotle and his friends would have looked upon someone who refused on principle to indulge in "wine, women, and song" as an insufferable bore. (Libertines and gluttons, at least, can be fun.) So, too, "friendliness" for Aristotle is not at all our slap-a-stranger-on-the-back-and-give-a big-smile variety. Friendliness refers more to *being* a friend than to any particular feeling or expression of friendship. It certainly does not mean being friendly to everybody.

Aristotle sometimes says that the good man has *all* the virtues, indeed, that one cannot have any of them without having all of them. Perhaps this assertion is overstated, but we understand what he means; having any virtue involves a certain good upbringing and self-control. (He refers to the virtues in general as "means between the extremes;" for example, courage is the mean between cowardice and foolhardiness.) A virtue, he says, "is a state of character." It is not merely doing the right thing at the right time, and it is not merely a passing passion. A virtue is an excellence that has been drilled into us since childhood and is now a matter of habit. Indeed, the idea that a person should struggle to be virtuous would strike Aristotle as nonsense; to have a virtue means that one acts virtuously naturally, without struggle, typically enjoying one's virtue rather than "forcing oneself to do it."

We might also notice that Aristotle's virtues are formulated around a certain kind of life; they are not virtues available to anyone. (Indeed, Aristotle thought that barbarians could not have any of the virtues because they did not live in so sophisticated a society as the Greek polis. He might well think that of us too.) The virtues listed by Aristotle are the virtues of aristocratic, male, Athenian citizens. Women in Athens did not have the freedom or the status to strive for such ideals. Slaves, of course, could be nothing more than "good slaves," according to Aristotle. Children were not to be called virtuous or happy; they were pre-adults, whose virtuousness and happiness could be judged only later. Indeed, many of the virtues of the craftsperson that we now consider admirable and important—being an excellent artist or musician, a fine cabinet maker or a productive farmer—are totally ignored by Aristotle. Such excellences are not worthy of the name "virtue" in a culture defined by its aristocracy and aristocratic virtues.

What is a virtue? David Hume describes the virtues as simply those characteristics which are useful or pleasing to us. Aristotle rather flatly describes them as those states of character which are conducive to "the good life for man," that is, for the Athenian aristocratic man. But a virtue is something more than useful or pleasing, and it is something more particular than a means to the good life for man, more general than a means to the good life for a Greek aristocrat. In his book, *After Virtue,* Alasdair MacIntyre provides us with an extensive analysis of the concept of virtue and the variety of virtues that we find in history from Homer to the Victorians. A virtue, he tells us, is not merely an admirable trait in a particular society. It is, rather, one of the cardinal features of what he calls a "practice," or, more generally, what we have been calling an ethos. The very notion of a virtue presupposes a set of ideals, a sense of what people in a particular society are supposed to strive for and admire. The virtues may be very rare in practice, as some Christian saints have exemplified; or they may be fairly common, as Aristotle considered the Athenian virtues to be among the aristocracy. But virtues are the ideals of a particular ethos, a part of its conception of its own ultimate purpose, or *telos.* Aristotle saw his society primarily in political terms, as an enlightened aristocracy whose members were trying to get on well with one another. A medieval monastery sees its telos in God, and its virtues are therefore piety and faith. We see ourselves as a society that maximizes happiness and efficiency, and our virtues, accordingly, tend to be psychological and economic (the "work ethic," for example). The virtues are, in general, useful to the society of which they are an essential part, but it would be a mistake to think that this is all that they are. A virtue may long outlive its usefulness and yet continue to play an essential role in the life of a community. And there may well be excellences that are essential to the life of a community which, for one reason or another, are never considered virtues. Aristotle's Athens had an agrarian economy, for example, but farming was never mentioned by him and was clearly "beneath" his ethical concerns.

VIRTUES AND VICES: DEFINING PRACTICES

Even in Aristotle's comparatively homogenous society, it would have been misleading to say that there is one set of virtues for everyone. His list is quite explicitly limited to that small class of male Athenian aristocrats whose role in the polis was leadership and statesmanship. There were other virtues for ordinary soldiers and for craftsmen, for wives, for slaves, and for farmers. In our pluralistic society, therefore, it would be absurd to think that there is a single set of virtues and vices for everyone, even if it is equally absurd to suggest, as many "self-help" psychology books do, that each of us has our own unique virtues that are ours alone.

Nevertheless, clearly there are certain clusters of virtues and vices which, while they may vary enormously with groups and persons, do cling dependably to practices of certain kinds. For example, there are scholarly virtues which are essential to studying and research:

• Being thorough: Sifting through all the evidence, reading as many books on the subject as possible, not neglecting available alternative hypotheses or interpretations
   Contrasting vice: Being neglectful, careless, or just plain ignorant
• Being thoughtful and organized: Having a thesis, planning ahead, and not just throwing together a lot of facts and figures that don't lead or add up to anything
   Contrasting vice: Being careless, disorganized
• Being profound or "deep": Having something to say that is new, surprising, or thought-provoking
   Contrasting vice: Being obvious or superficial
• Being clear: Presenting your research so that it is easily understood
   Contrasting vice: Being obscure
• Being serious: Thinking that what one is doing, no matter how precious or irrelevant, is important. Humor has its place perhaps, but never concerning the worth of the study itself
   Contrasting vice: Lacking seriousness
• Being honest: Giving proper credit for sources and stating the facts as you find them, not making them up as you need them
   Contrasting vice: Being dishonest

and, last but not least,

- Saying what is true, or at least plausible
  Contrasting vice: Being wrong, or worse, trite or ridiculous

These intellectual virtues and vices define the practice that we call scholarship. We can, of course, think of quite different enterprises going under the same name. Among them, for example, are grubbing for grades or groping for tenure, but, within the practice, these are clearly distortions and perversions of it, with virtues and vices quite opposed to the scholarly virtues—in this case, the desire to please professorial authority at any cost. True scholars will manifest most of these virtues most of the time, but their part in the practice of scholarship depends on the recognition as well as the exemplification of these virtues and the condemnation of these vices. Indeed, within the practice, the scholar will not even consider the notion that there might be opposed virtues, or that some seeming vices (such as carelessness or spontaneity) might in fact be virtues. As part of another practice, perhaps they might be, but scholarship is defined by the practice of careful, thorough, honest pursuit of the truth. The virtues are those characteristics that make a person an admirable participant in this practice: the vices are those that make one less than admirable, if they don't eliminate the possessor from the practice altogether.

So, too, we could define a list of virtues and vices in the arts (being creative versus being imitative, being emotionally moving versus being boring, being technically competent as opposed to incompetent, having taste versus having bad or no taste, being pure versus "selling out"); in athletics (being or not being a good player, trying hard versus "goofing off," trying to win versus not caring, cooperating with the team versus being just "out for one's own glory," being a good sport versus being a bad sport); in romance (being attractive versus unattractive, suave and stylish vers s clumsy and vulgar, considerate versus selfish, sensuous versus insensitive, sexually exciting versus boring or gross); and in business (being enterprising versus lazy, shrewd versus foolish, honest versus dishonest, foresightful versus behind the times, profitable versus bankrupt). In each of these practices and in many more besides, we can see how the virtues are in every case aimed at excellence in the practice; the vices, if allowed to flourish, would defeat or destroy the practice. One can't have scholarship without concern for the truth; one can't have art without concern for creativity and an insistence on "good taste"; and one can't have sports without good sportsmanship. One can't have romance without sensuality and suaveness; one can't have business without shrewdness and profits, but neither can one have business without honesty and respect for contracts and one's word. The virtues define the practice and those who have the virtues carry on the practice. Those who have the vices, on the other hand, are systematically chastized or thrown out of the practice for the sake of the survival of the practice itself. Of course, practices can change, and they can go out of existence, too. But every practice has its virtues and vices, and those who make up the practice will be those with the virtues, not those with the vices. There are practices which are themselves defined by vice—organized crime and prostitution, for example; nevertheless, within the practice, there is still a crucial distinction between what is acceptable behavior and what is not.

Among the virtues and vices of these particular practices, certain ones keep repeating themselves, for example, the virtue of honesty and the vice of dishonesty, which appear (or could be included) in every one of the practices mentioned in the previous paragraph. The reappearance of such common qualities in many different practices suggests that over and above the list of virtues and vices for each particular practice, there is also an all-encompassing list of virtues and vices that define all practices. This, however, could be misleading. There are virtues and vices which, if defined broadly enough, may be included in most, if not all, practices, but the very breadth of the definition makes them obscure. Then we face the problem, What practice defines these super virtues and vices? It will not do merely to say, "Being a human being," for this in itself is not a practice. Indeed, one becomes a human being only when one enters a culture and participates in its practices. Nor will it do to say blandly, "Being a good person," for there are a great many people who are excellent in particular practices but are not thereby "good people."

This idea of super virtues and vices suggests that, in addition to such particular practices as the above, there is a more general practice which we expect everyone in our society to respect. We might call this practice "mutual tolerance and consideration," that is, the overall practice that puts the other practices into perspective and protects them from one another. The practices of art and scholarship, not to mention those of sports and romance, may be threatened by the infiltration of business practices, and all the practices can be threatened by the infiltration of violence and disrespect for the practice itself. (Imagine a maniac in an art gallery or a psychopathic heckler in a philosophy lecture, a fan with a gun in a sporting match or a Don Juan or Doña Juanita who considers love nothing but a ploy to conquer people.) Thus, such virtues as honesty and such vices as dishonesty still derive their meaning within the practices they help define, but they also have a more general meaning: they are the virtues that allow us to have practices in the first place, without falling into a "free-for-all" in which there are no rules, no sense of shared enterprise, and no cooperation, in which nothing ever gets done (nor, indeed, would anyone even know what is to be done). The vices, by contrast, are those states of character that destroy the availability of practices and tend to reduce all our practices to chaos. It is not surprising, therefore, that such characteristics as disrespect for the rules, selfishness, and dishonesty turn out to be vices in almost every practice, for they destroy the practice.

One way of talking about this general set of virtues and vices is to call them "moral" virtues (and "immoral" vices). Aristotle distinguishes between what he calls "moral" and "intellectual" virtues—the former having to do with our practical behavior in society (the list we presented in the preceding section), the latter relating to thinking and understanding (a broad version of what we called the "scholarly" virtues). The moral virtues, in this sense, are those which are generally conducive to our coherence as a society; in our pluralist society, this means, first and foremost, our willingness to respect practices other than our own as well as our participation in both particular practices (such as scholarship, romance, and sports) and the general practice of freely participating in different practices.

The generality of moral virtues can lead to a familiar extravagance, however: the supposition that there is a single set of virtues and vices that define good and bad people. We can agree, of course, that someone who is selfish, inconsiderate, disrespectful of all rules, indifferent to considerations of fairness, honesty, truth, and taste is disastrously destructive to all practices and to the participation in practices in general. There is, however, a significant number of virtues which, while intolerable in a great number of people, are nevertheless important in some. One example is the "wise guy," the person who, while participating in a practice (and participating in it much more seriously than he seems to) also makes fun of it and disrupts it. Several "wise guys" would destroy any practice (even the practice of being a "wise guy"), but just one such person allows everyone else to relax a bit and get a perspective on this practice that might otherwise be lost. Another example is the eccentric genius who risks being ostracized and being made fun of for wanting to take a practice beyond its current limits. Again, no practice can consist wholly of eccentrics, even geniuses (thus the absurdity, for example, of a "village idiots'" convention), but a few geniuses keep a practice alive and invigorating. To insist that the virtues consist of those characteristics that everyone should have in a practice or in a society with a plurality of practices is to miss the importance of these exceptions. But, at the same time, to insist that everyone be an exception and to celebrate only the eccentric virtues is an equal absurdity. The virtues are as varied as our practices, and it is the variety of characters and practices that we consider, as a society (and as individuals) to be our greatest virtue.

DUTY, SAINTS, HEROES, AND ROGUES

Much of what is discussed under the title of "morality" has to do with fulfilling obligations, with doing one's duty—what one *ought* to do. But, although our basic conception of morality is bound up with obeying principles and not breaking moral rules, there is another source and another meaning of morality which are all too easily neglected, perhaps because they are so obvious. We learn morality, and we learn what morality is, first of all not by principle but by *example.* As children, we are told to "look at how well your big sister is behaving herself," and we are inundated with stories and movies which feature moral examples, everything from lessons in manners on "Sesame Street" to demonstrations of virtue in Shakespeare, the usual stories about George Washington and Abraham Lincoln to the mundane morality tales of daily television. From ancient times, we have had the heroes of the *Iliad* and, in philosophy, Socrates; the Bible is full of heroes and examples of goodness, and of evil too. Indeed, the pronouncement of principles plays but a small role in our moral education; imitation and emulation are far more powerful, just because they are far more personal and substantial.

We have already noted that one problem with a conception of morality which is limited to obeying the rules of the "thou shalt not. . ." variety is that a perfectly good person might also be an absolute bore, a moral prig whose behavior benefits no one and inspires no one. The consequence of such a conception is that morality becomes a dreary, quite boring, and tedious affair. The "antimoralist" Nietzsche thus suggests that morality is essentially a "leveling" device intended to lop off the peaks of human excellence as well as to raise up the "herd" to a "higher" form of behavior. Extraordinary behavior, heroic and saintly deeds, would be ignored in such a conception, and, indeed, moral theorists in the Kantian mold have been hard-pressed to give an adequate account of those who go far beyond their moral duties to display such extraordinary behavior. A special term has been provided for such behavior which is "beyond the call of duty": *supererogatory*. But any word in ethics that is seven syllables long is suspicious; this one converts those exemplary acts and people making up the very heart of ethics into a curious and problematic set of exceptions.

We can better understand the nature of these inspiring examples in the terms we have just been discussing—the ethics of virtue and the virtues instead of a morality of obedience to principles. Indeed, it is the primary datum of ethics, not a set of exceptions, that there are people who go far beyond the rules, not breaking them but far exceeding their demands. It is significant, for example, that Aristotle's ethics turns on the crucial concept of *excellence.* The good man, for Aristotle, is not just one who obeys the rules; he also excels in what he does. This is not to say that he disobeys the rules and laws of Athenian society; he just does not often think of them—they are "second nature" to him. What he concentrates on is excelling. He is expected not only not to flee from battle; he is expected to fight to the best of his ability. He is not only expected not to lie (which is easy enough if you keep silent); he is also expected to be witty and clever and informative, if not as brilliant as Socrates. Ethics, in other words, need not be confined to obedient mediocrity. It is also the demand for excellence—and more.

This idea of going *beyond* morality, beyond the "call of duty," is nowhere more evident than in those special people whom we designate as *saints* and *heroes.* A saint is not just someone who is perfectly good in the easy sense of not sinning (perhaps not having had any opportunities); a saint is extraordinarily good, resisting temptations that we cannot imagine resisting and doing good deeds that are far beyond the demands of duty or charity. Similarly, a hero or heroine is a person who does not do just what is commanded, but much more—indeed, much more than anyone could have expected. One cannot command saintliness or heroism, and it is no one's duty to be a saint or a hero or heroine. Nevertheless, our ethics would be impoverished without such concepts and we aspire to *be* such persons even if we are limited to occasional fantasies and unrealistic self-criticism. This aspiration inspires the best in us and the best of what we call our morals. Refraining from a forbidden act because of fear of punishment or anticipation of guilt may still count as "moral," but it is nothing like, and does not feel at all like, that sense of what Nietzsche calls "nobility" which motivates our best actions. Acting from a sense of duty may be motivated and accompanied by a comforting sense of righteousness, but that is something less than even the beginning of sainthood or heroism, for it is typical of the saint and the hero that they do not even think of what they are doing in such terms. Indeed, it is in part that naiveté, devoid of self-doubt and deliberation, that may make them saints and heroes.

Saints and heroes have the virtues appropriate to their cultures; these will not, obviously, all be the same. The Christian saints had different virtues from those of the Buddha, and Saint Francis had different virtues from Mohammed's. Achilles and Alexander the Great had very different virtues from those of Gandhi and Martin Luther King, and Einstein, who was a popular folk hero in America, had a different set of virtues from those of Giordano Bruno, who was burned at the stake in 1600 for his scientific speculations. But the virtues of the saints and heroes are not just the ordinary virtues that make a "good person"—honesty, trustworthiness, a sense of humor; indeed, their virtues may be such as to eclipse some of those more ordinary and domesticated virtues altogether, particularly in times of moral turmoil when saints and heroes are particularly prevalent. It is far more important to the sainthood of Augustine that he was extremely devout than that he had a sense of humor, and it is far more important to the heroism of Beowulf that he could slay terrifying monsters than that he should be a "nice guy."

The occasional contradiction between virtues and moral rules, between the virtues themselves and in particular between the more ordinary virtues and the extraordinary virtues of saints and heroes helps to explain an ethical phenomenon which we mentioned only briefly in Part One—the example of the "rogue." Rogues are familiar heroes and heroines in contemporary American literature and culture, even if they have not yet made a noticeable appearance in ethics as such. The rogue is almost always a likable figure, often played in movies by such charming stars as Burt Reynolds and Goldie Hawn, for example. Typically, the rogue character breaks the law, or at least is at odds with the law, having robbed a bank or undertaken some devious, daredevil plot which more often than not, in American movies, includes breaking no fewer than several dozen traffic laws within a ten-minute chase scene. In literary criticism, such a character is often called the "antihero," a term that expresses some ethical confusion about the fact that the person has the status but not the morals of a hero.

Why should such a character be mentioned in ethics at all, except perhaps as an unfortunate popular example of rampant immorality? Because, first of all, like it or not, these are the "heroes" and "heroines" who now provide the moral examples for millions of American children. (Burt Reynolds was voted both the most popular and the most admired male in America in several youth polls over the past few years—not Reynolds the private individual, of course, but Reynolds as the "bandit" persona of the movies.) Second, such examples illustrate quite clearly the complexity of our actual morals and moral conceptions, which are not limited to universal rules and obedience but, quite the contrary, include a distinctive admiration for those who dare to be different—so long as they are also charming and attractive. Third, it points out the enormous range of the concept of "character" in ethics, which is not restricted to the traditional "man (or woman) of character" of Victorian novels—a person who is honorable, trustworthy, and a good mate; it also includes eccentrics and rogues who are not at all "moral" in the narrow, traditional sense.

It would be misleading, however, to leave the example of the rogue in the hands of American moviemakers, as if the sole occupation of such characters were the perpetration of financially rewarding felonies. There is a far more honorable history of roguery, in which the compensating virtues go beyond superficial charm and attractiveness and provide rewards for society for generations to come. This history includes many of the great artists of past centuries who were famously difficult people and often selfish and immoral as well. (Whether they had to be so to be great artists, or became so because they were great artists, are two much-celebrated but dubious hypotheses which we need not explore here.) Beethoven, for example, scandalized most of Viennese society with his lack of manners and the absence of any sense of trustworthiness. The great French author Balzac motivated himself to write by plunging deeply in debt with high living. Picasso's moral eccentricities have been much publicized in recent years, but his behavior is not very different from that of a great many famous artists—male and female—in the bohemian culture in which the arts have flourished for the past century or so. In the realm of the intellect, Freud and Jung have often been accused of inconsiderate if not immoral behavior toward their psychoanalytic colleagues. Even Martin Luther has often been portrayed as a man who was deeply neurotic, frequently inconsistent if not hypocritical, and cruel to many of those closest to him. And yet, given the enormous contributions of these "rogues" to our culture, it seems beside the point to dwell on their personal failings. Indeed, we virtually expect to find "dirt" on almost every genius whose life we study, and we are far more surprised when we find an exemplary and unblemished life than we are when we discover, once again, that our moral heroes were not always moral.

Our point here is not to defend "immorality." It should be noted that the behavior of rogues is rarely immoral in any repulsive sense; otherwise, they would quickly lose their status as "heroes" of any kind. It is to make the point once again that our ethics is a complex and flexible system of concerns, as complex and as flexible as our pluralistic ethos. Indeed, one reason for stressing that the rogue is important to us is to emphasize this pluralism. (Another reason for the popularity of rogues in many societies is their attack on corrupt or unreasonable authority.) Thus, despite occasional immorality or criminality, the rogue may represent to us some of the virtues most prized in our society—independence, humor, initiative, a kind of courage. To think of the rogue as simply "immoral," therefore, is to miss an extremely important ethical point. And to focus on a single moral example, such as "the good person" who exemplifies Kant's insistence on "a good will" with good intentions and respect for duty and other people as ends, is to paint an emaciated picture of ethics and present a fraudulent portrait of our *ethos*.

JUSTICE AND EQUALITY

Of all the virtues, perhaps the most prominent—in both the good society and in the moral individual—is *justice*. Socrates, Plato, and Aristotle, for example, praise it more than any other virtue and devote an extraordinary amount of attention to it. Justice is the defining feature of social and political philosophy because it is an essential concern of governments and social critics and planners. But it is also essential to ethics, to our sense of "fair play" and correct behavior in personal transactions. To be just is one of the cardinal virtues of both Christianity and ancient paganism, and it is still one of those virtues which is most characteristic of the "good person."

There are several aspects of justice, but two in particular command our attention: *retributive* justice and *distributive* justice. Retributive justice is essentially concerned with punishments, with assigning blame and punishing people in proportion to their misdeeds. Distributive justice is, rather, concerned with the distribution of the goods of society, in part as a matter of reward but also in accordance with needs and a number of other factors. The two kinds of justice are often treated independently, but they share common structures and concepts, in particular the concept of "fairness" and the importance of the notion of *equality*. In retributive justice, it is considered to be of the utmost importance that everyone be treated fairly and as "equals before the law." A poor man is not to be punished more harshly than a rich man, and the punishment for a traffic violation should never be more severe than a punishment for felonious assault. In distributive justice, it is extremely important that a person be rewarded in accordance with what he or she deserves, and two people doing the same job equally well deserve the same salaries. To treat people unequally for irrelevant reasons—to punish a man or pay him less because he is black, for example—is a flagrant violation of justice. Fairness and equality thus become the central features of justice and the source of its most difficult problems too.

What is fair, and how do we know? To begin with, we feel reasonably certain about many cases of *in*justice: the case of a father who receives the death sentence for stealing a loaf of bread for his starving children, the innocent student who is singled out for punishment as an example for the entire class, the enormous raise in salary given to the boss's nephew, who hasn't shown up for work in a month. And in each example, we can begin to formulate reasons for thinking: here is a case of unfairness. The punishment should fit the crime and "extenuating circumstances" should be considered, such as a father's desperate attempt to save his children (contrasted, for instance, with a selfish individual stealing just for the fun of it). In the second case, our initial hypothesis might well be that blame should be restricted to those who actually did something wrong. No matter how effective making an example of an innocent student may be, we feel that it is unfair to punish someone who is not in fact to blame. In the third case, we feel quite strongly that a person should get a reward only after earning it, and that being the boss's nephew is no entitlement to special treatment. Indeed, it is no reason for him to get the job in the first place.

The notion of fairness does not provide much of a definition of justice, if only because we so often use the words "fairness" and "justice" interchangeably. But fairness, in general, points to an agreeable "fit" between rewards and punishments and right and wrong actions, between what we do and what we expect we *ought* to do. To break the agreed-upon rules of a game is unfair; to break a promise is, among other things, unfair too. To punish an innocent person is unfair, but so is a punishment which is much more serious than the crime, and so is a punishment that is much less severe than the crime (though the criminal will rarely complain). To allow anyone to starve in the streets in a prosperous country strikes many people as grossly unfair, and for "the rich to get richer while the poor get poorer" is also a paradigm case of unfairness to a great many people who nevertheless have no doubts about the virtues of being rich and getting richer.

At the core of our conception of both justice and fairness, however, lies the principle of equality: Every person has equal worth and is to be treated the same in terms of rewards and punishments. It is worth noting that this has not always been the core of justice, however. Most societies have divided people into castes or classes and given more of the goods of society to one group (usually the aristocracy, the priesthood, or the military) than to other groups (often the peasants and menial workers). Plato's *Republic,* for example, makes very clear that different groups are to be treated very differently in the ideal society (as they were indeed in his own less-than-ideal society). Aristotle even defends slavery in his *Politics* and suggests that slaves are "naturally" unequal to Greek citizens and therefore deserving of few of the benefits available to Athenian citizens. Nevertheless, it is significant that Aristotle, too, mentions "equality" as one of the concepts central to justice, not in the sense that everyone is essentially the same (which he would have considered utter nonsense), but in the sense that justice is a matter of "balance" and "proportion," and that "it does not matter whether it is a good man or a bad man who has committed adultery; the law looks only to the distinctive character of the injury, and treats the parties as equal" (*Nicomachean Ethics,* chapter 5). Thus Aristotle takes "equality under the law" to be essential to justice, even while rejecting much of what we would consider essential to equality.

What is equality? It is not, we can be sure, the claim that everyone makes equally valuable contributions to society and, in that sense, is of equal worth. We can all agree, for example, that a medical genius who invents one lifesaving device after another is worth far more than a hoodlum from a spoiled childhood who vents his Oedipal rage by "mugging" one law-abiding citizen after another. The claim of equal worth is often said to depend on the dubious notion that people are basically the same, with the same abilities and capacities to live a good life and contribute to society. But this sentimental sense of equality is obviously false as soon as we begin to think about it; some people are born with intelligence, and some are tragically "retarded." Some people are born healthy, others are sickly or crippled for life. Some people are reared in loving homes with good examples of happiness all around them; others are raised in misery, and misery seems to be built into them. A student who works his or her way through the local urban night school with mediocre grades because of having to work all day may never be in a position to make the dramatic contributions to society possible for the well-bred Harvard graduate who is born into political connections and power. We might well say that each of these students will make contributions to the best of his or her ability. But isn't this very much like Plato's quite inegalitarian society, where different people are thought of and treated very differently according to their varying abilities and opportunities, and so are not equal at all?

Consider the case of education in a democratic society, where the issue of equality is brought very much into focus. Is there any sense in giving two children the same educational opportunities when one, with proper training, will obviously learn a great deal, while the other, even with an exhausting effort, will learn very little? Of course, we could be wrong. Apparent potential frequently turns out to be disappointing, and the dolt in the back of the class occasionally emerges as a great scholar or scientist. (Einstein flunked high school math.) Perhaps we should say that all students deserve *equal opportunity,* but does this mean that everyone should receive exactly the same education (which usually cheats very good and very poor students alike), or does it mean that everyone should receive the education which will be of greatest personal benefit? But then, of course, they will be treated very differently—and at very different costs—and not educated equally at all. What does equal opportunity mean, unless all students actually begin their education with the same skills and encouragement? What if some students begin with severe disadvantages? If the worst students cannot utilize the same opportunities as the best students, should the better students therefore be penalized? (In a perverse short story, Kurt Vonnegut suggests an intricate system of handicaps—to make strong people weaker, graceful people clumsy, beautiful people plain, and smart people distracted—all in the name of "equality.")

It has proven to be very difficult to formulate a notion of equality that is not hopelessly vague and that will do the important political work we want it to do. Nevertheless, we remain adamant that some notion of equality is essential to justice, that people should not only be treated similarly by the law for the crimes they commit, but also be given equal opportunities for advancement and the good life. But equality is not the only factor in our notion of justice, even in our unusually egalitarian society. We also insist that people get what they deserve—punishment for their crimes, rewards for their contributions—and in this sense, we insist on treating people unequally. (*If* two people commit the same crimes or make the same contributions, however, *then* we insist that they be treated the same.) We summarize this aspect of justice with the word "*merit*": people make different contributions and so deserve different rewards from society. We also insist that, even if people do not contribute as much to society as we would like, they should be rewarded (or punished) for *effort* (or lack of it), since we recognize that hard work should be rewarded (and laziness punished) even if it is not always successful (or harmful). We also believe that people should be rewarded for setting an example, whether or not they personally produce anything as such, and that people in positions of responsibility deserve extraordinary reward, just by virtue of their visibility and responsibility. Clearly we, as a society, believe that it is just for people in sports or entertainment, who sometimes have little talent, to be rewarded in terms of both wealth and fame far more lavishly than virtually any other working people. We also believe that people should be rewarded, sometimes extravagantly, for taking risks (and not always very great risks), for example, when they invest money in the stock market or real estate, whether or not they are thereby supporting any useful enterprise. We also believe that justice *entitles* people to certain goods, whether or not they have worked for or earned them in any way. We would consider it unjust, for example, if a father decided to give his entire fortune to his old college roommate—no matter how deserving—and cut his infant son off without a cent to pay his future college tuition and get him started in life. We might object, of course, to what we consider excessive advantages and abuses of inheritance, but our sense of justice clearly includes some sense of entitlement to what one should inherit. Finally, it is clear that we believe that justice also requires the care of those who cannot care for themselves, whether or not we would go as far as the classic Marxist conception of justice: "From each according to (his) abilities; to each according to (his) needs."

Many of the moral virtues and many of the demands of morality refer primarily to the activities or character of the individual. Justice, on the other hand, has to do with the interchange of life, giving and taking, sharing and refusing to share, punishing and being punished by others for our trespasses and crimes, giving rewards and praise and receiving them for the things that we do for others. It is, we might say, the virtue that holds society together, whether or not— as has been suggested—love (*agape*) might ideally do the job as well.

RIGHTS

On the high side of ethics is the good life, the life filled with pleasures, successes, love, friendship, good health, considerable comfort and luxuries as well as virtues and moral rectitude, a sense of justice heightened, perhaps, by the fact that one has oneself done so well. But on the down side of ethics is the life led by those millions who are not so fortunate, for whom misery and failure are more familiar than pleasure and success. Not everyone is lovable; indeed, not everyone has a friend. Good health is the advantage of a minority of the human medical specimens on earth, and comforts, certainly luxuries, are not common to all. Justice is, in part, the concern for those who are not so well off as ourselves, through no fault of their own. But, in addition to our compassion and concern, there is another ingredient in the down side of ethics: the *rights* of those less fortunate, their legitimate claims against those who have come so much closer to the good life than they have or ever will.

A right is first of all a *claim,* a *demand* of sorts, which is made by one person on another (or on an entire society). Every right, therefore, has a correlative *obligation*: one person has a right while the other (or society) has the obligation. For example, every person in our society has a constitutionally guaranteed right to freedom of speech, which means that everyone else (and the government) has the obligation not to infringe upon that right. Moreover, many people would insist that every member of our society has a right to a decent job and a good education (though these are not guaranteed by the Constitution); it is therefore the obligation of society (though not, usually, of particular individuals or groups) to provide jobs and education. To use a term we briefly employed in our previous discussion of justice, we might say that a right is an *entitlement,* a legitimate demand such that one is *entitled* to freedom of speech, a decent job, and a good education.

There are different kinds of rights. Some rights, such as those guaranteed by the Constitution or other laws of the land, are *legal rights,* rights by virtue of law. Such rights, however, are clearly relative to a particular society and its laws. A man has a right to marry many wives in some societies, not in others. Women have the right to vote and smoke in public in some cultures, not in others. But we would not want to say that the rights guaranteed by our Constitution, in particular, are rights merely by virtue of the law. We want to say that they are rights essential to our society, whether or not they are canonized in law. (Thus, the right to a decent job is a right essential to our "work ethic" society, but it is not guaranteed by law.) Such rights, which are essential to the nature of a certain society, are often called *civil rights*. Such basic aspects of our society as its belief in equality, for example, are manifested in such civil rights as the right not to face discrimination by virtue of race or religion or sex. Not surprisingly, these civil rights are typically written into law, and thus become legal rights as well.

Civil rights are still relative to the customs of a particular society, however. Although this suits us quite well when the rights at stake seem to us to be matters of custom rather than matters of morality, there are certain rights that appear to us to deserve *universal* status, like the principles of morality. These are called *human rights* (they used to be called "natural rights") because they apply to all human beings everywhere, regardless of the customs of their particular societies. For example, the right not to be tortured is generally agreed to be such a right. It does not matter whether it is written into law or part of the culture of a society. Torture is a violation of rights. So too, according to the United Nations Declaration of 1948, every person on earth has the human right to "social security . . . and a standard of living adequate for health and well-being." Of course, what counts as "health and well-being" has been a topic of considerable debate, and the dramatic advances in medical technology raise very difficult questions about the extent to which everyone could possibly have the right to receive the best medical treatment available, since it is in fact "available" only to one person in a million, and at enormous cost. Nevertheless, the idea of human rights—notably, the right not to be imprisoned without reason and the right not to be tortured—is essential to our ethics. For, however much emphasis we may put on the quest for the good life, we are also aware that there are more minimal but more urgent demands being claimed by those less fortunate than we are. Recognition of others' rights is as essential to our conception of the good life as morality. Indeed, recognition of the rights of others has been cited by some contemporary philosophical authors as the very foundation of morality.

We can divide up the hierarchy of rights, from the most basic human rights to the most specific and sometimes trivial legal rights (for example, the right of high school students to wear jeans to class) in another way. We can call these *freedom rights* and *entitlement rights,* respectively, and we might notice that they display a parallel to the distinction between "negative" and "positive" freedom which we discussed in an earlier section. Freedom (or negative) rights are rights not to be interfered with, rights "to be left alone." The right to freedom of speech, the right to privacy, the right to worship as one chooses, the right to choose one's friends and travel where one wishes: these are all freedom rights, in which other people and the government are obliged to leave us alone. Entitlement (or positive) rights are those which allow a person to make a legitimate claim to get some good from others (or from the society as a whole). The most familiar example on an individual level is the outcome of a promise or a contract; by virtue of having been promised or guaranteed something in writing, one has a right to receive whatever it is that was promised or contracted. Entitlement rights concerning the goods of society as a whole—for example, the rights to medical care, decent jobs, housing, and education—may similarly be viewed as "promises" of the society to each and every individual within it. Indeed, there is a popular theory of society which says that people have rights in society just because there is an implicit "social contract" in which every citizen has been promised certain benefits. (We sometimes forget that the same "contract" extracts, in return, a number of promises from us that we serve society and make sacrifices.)

The concept of rights is often and easily abused. When the ethics of a society is so defined by rights as ours is, the temptation to extend the notion of a "right" to everything that one wants is almost unavoidable. Thus, because we want the good life, we tend to think that we are entitled to it, and because we are so used to freedom in so many aspects of life, we tend to think that we have the right not to be interfered with in any instance, no matter how disruptive or obnoxious or even dangerous we may be. But a right is a particularly precious part of ethics just because rights are so basic and are concerned with those essential, minimal conditions without which a decent life is not even possible. Thus it is more than just self-indulgence when someone insists on a right to blast a tape deck on a bus or smoke in a crowded theater. It is an abuse of one of the most basic concepts of our ethos.

PART FOUR

FOUR

THE JUSTIFICATION
OF MORALITY

THE UNREASONABLE QUESTION: WHY BE MORAL?

Morality, as opposed to prudence and pure selfishness, is wholly concerned with doing what one *ought* to do, with behaving in the socially prescribed way and obeying principles. To be moral, therefore, is to put one's own interests in a secondary position, sometimes sacrificing one's interests altogether for the sake of "morality." But why, someone is bound to ask, must a person be moral? Why should one ever act against one's own interests—unless, of course, doing so is also in one's interests (in the long run, for example)? What reasons will motivate a person to be moral? Can morality itself be justified?

The question itself is, in an important sense, unreasonable. Morality and moral considerations *are* the justifications of our (moral) acts. "Because it was the right thing to do" and "Because I promised him that I would" are usually definitive justifications for action. The primary reason for doing the moral act is precisely that it is moral. Indeed, many philosophers, especially Kant, have said that being moral and being rational—that is, acting for the right reasons—are one and the same. To ask, "Why be moral?" is therefore to ask, in effect, "Why should I do the right thing for the right reasons?" or simply, "Why should I be reasonable?" What kind of answer is possible? Cambridge philosopher Bernard Williams dismisses the person who would ask such a question as a psychopath. Less philosophical defenders of morality suggest rather a spanking or a long-term prison sentence. Nevertheless, given the importance of morality in our ethics, it would seem that the question Why be moral? ought

101

to have an answer—and a roundly convincing one. Why is it so difficult to pin it down?

The most plausible answer to the unreasonable question is the circular one: One *ought* to be moral because obligation is what the word "moral" means. The moral way of behaving is, by definition, the *right* way. Indeed, Kant formulates his entire ethical strategy around his view that the correctness of morals is already given to us ("Two things forever fill me with awe, the starry skies above and the moral law within"). The task of ethics, therefore, is not to justify morality to the skeptic who asks the unreasonable question; it is, rather, to show *why* morality has the authority it does, which is the same as showing how and why it is the necessary expression of "practical reason." Many ethicists in recent years have undertaken a similar strategy; they don't actually respond to the unreasonable question but, rather, give an *analysis* of the terms "good," "moral," and "reasons," confident that such a "metaethical" analysis will show why moral considerations have such importance for us. The logic of this strategy, though not usually stated as such, is to assume that we all do, in fact, acknowledge the authority of morality and its reasons. The unreasonable question is therefore reinterpreted in a more innocent way as the request for an elaboration on what it is to give a moral reason.

Even if we are indeed moral and not psychopathic, however, such analyses are not satisfying. We do want to hear an adequate reply to moral skeptics and their unreasonable question. Indeed, this is not merely theoretical persistence. Most of us occasionally find ourselves in a situation in which the persuasiveness of morality is rendered wobbly or worse by the desperation or attractiveness of an isolated, but most immoral, situation. ("I wouldn't do this generally, of course, but—just this once....") The money is just lying there for the taking, or you've never met anyone so attractive in your life, married or not, or the Internal Revenue Service will never be able to trace this little claim. The temptations are there. It would be helpful, to say the least, if we knew the reason why we ought to resist. We already know that the act is "wrong." What we want from ethics is something more than that, a *justification* of morality, not just a restatement of it.

Suppose a person will accept the justification of morality *only* if it also shows that being moral is in his or her self-interest? Could we provide such a justification? Would we thereby justify morality, or would we, instead, show (as the skeptic would be quick to point out) that there is, strictly speaking, no morality, only self-interest? What if a person refuses to listen to justification at all and simply insists on doing whatever he or she wants to do? Short of physical threats (which never count as an argument in philosophy), are there any reasons which should be ultimately convincing? And, as we search for such reasons, we should also reflectively ask, "What are we doing when we try to justify morality?" Are we trying to convince someone who refuses to be moral?

Or are we mainly trying to reassure ourselves? Where do our doubts come from in the first place? (Surely they did not originate in a philosophy class.)

ACTING FOR REASONS: TWO KINDS OF THEORIES

The key to morality and its justification is that we do not just act; we act for *reasons*. Indeed, it is the very nature of human action—as such diverse ethicists as Kant and Jean-Paul Sartre have shown—that it is *intentional,* which means that it is (1) purposive and (2) done for reasons. Whether or not we have an "intention" in mind before acting, our actions are rational and for reasons (even our irrational actions), and these reasons can (usually) be stated more or less clearly and without hesitation. Only in the exceptional case do we have to ponder the difficult question, "Why did I do that?"(It is only under the pressure of the pain of neurosis or the prodding of a psychoanalyst that one speculates on a psyche full of intentions which one never would have suspected without reading Freud.)

Dogs act with a purpose, of course; Fido scratches at the screen door *in order to* attract attention and be let out. But dogs don't act for reasons in the sense that is relevant to ethics, and, accordingly, even the best-behaved dog does not deserve to be called "moral." It is not just that reasons in ethics should be articulate, thus requiring language. (This traditional criterion for distinguishing between "man and beast" may well be both unfair and false.) It is, rather, that reasons require Reason, which is to say, a complex of reasons beyond the immediate "do this to get that." A college woman with the ambition to be a federal judge someday has to think in terms of years or decades, not just in terms of "wanting to get into law school" (in the sense in which the dog at the door of the law building "wants to get into law school"). She has to think in terms of her education, her credentials, her reputation, her choice of friends, the way she will spend her summers. And, to say the obvious, she must have a concept of "the law" and "the legal system," which would not be comprehensible to even the brightest German shepherd dog.

There is nothing in this complex of reasons that need be particularly moral, of course. Indeed, the young woman's ambition may have wholly to do with her own vision of herself, perhaps "to show them" back in Wichita Falls. But such an ambition is a clear example of how conceptually rich it is to act intentionally, to act for reasons. And it should also be clear that, apart from grabbing a Big Mac at the local fast-food counter, a great many of our actions have such conceptual richness, and so the question, "For what reason?" applies in a much larger sense than "Why is the dog scratching at the door again?"

To act for reasons means that the question of justification is relevant and important. It is not just an annoying addendum that philosophers have added to human action; it is part and parcel of human action as such. We would be shocked, to say the least, if the question, "Why do you want to go to law school?" were answered simply by, "Oh, I have no idea whatever" or "It just sounds like fun." Actions have reasons, and these reasons in turn have reasons. One applies to law school to get into law school, which one does in order to become a lawyer, which one does in order, perhaps, to enter politics, make money, join one's mother's law firm, etc. Ethics, then, can be considered the study of our reasons, and, indeed, much of what we have done in the previous three parts of the book is to explore the range and kinds of reasons that enter into ethics.

Reasoning and justification must have an end, however. There must be a terminus, a final purpose, a *telos.* A chain of reasons needs to be anchored; the network of reasons has to be hung somewhere. One might say, for example, that the ultimate reason for going to law school, or for doing anything, for that matter, is to be happy. Or to get more pleasure out of life. Or to become as powerful or as popular as possible. Such final ends provide the end of our reasoning. Indeed, if the skeptic returns with another unreasonable question, such as "Why do you want to be happy?" we seem stuck for an answer. Perhaps we can mumble something like "It's just human nature to want to be happy" or "Well, everyone wants to be happy." But, again, we have the feeling that the question is unreasonable. One does not, after all, question ultimate ends—and certainly not happiness.

The above candidates for the position of ultimate end of action and anchor for our reasons are, whatever their differences, all of a kind. They are all ultimate *purposes,* desirable ends in themselves toward which all our other actions and reasons are aimed. But there is another kind of reason, and another kind of terminus to our reasoning. The most prominent example, in our context, is "because it is the right way to live." "Because it is the moral thing to do" is another example of such a reason; "because God wills it" is still another. How are these reasons different from those mentioned previously? For one thing, ethicists would point out that they are not *personal* reasons in the way that happiness, pleasure, popularity, and power are; they are goods (even the Good) independently of people's wanting them. Other ethicists would therefore say that they are distinguished by their being *objective* reasons. But what is most immediately obvious about them is that they are all *moral* reasons, that is, they already presuppose the vocabulary and the viewpoint of the language of "right and wrong," "good and evil," "moral and immoral," "ought" and "obligation." It is evident that such reasons are involved in many of our actions, whether or not we are called upon to justify ourselves. That fact is not challenged even by moral skeptics, and their question, "Why be moral?" does not suggest that we do not, in reality, use such reasons and act according to them. The question challenges the ultimate justification of such reasons, that is, the idea that the chain of moral reasons can be anchored.

We have noted that the same question can be asked of the personal purposes above, as in "Why do you want to be happy?" But the moral skeptic—and most of us—would be quite willing to continue in our quest for happiness, or pleasure, or popularity, or power, even if we were not convinced that there were any more ultimate purpose in doing so. But this is not so clear where morality is the end. We are moral, presumably, because we assume that there is some higher reason for being so than our own personal well-being, or because we assume that being moral will also maximize our personal well-being. If morality is unjustifiable in either of these senses, there may indeed be no answer to the "unreasonable" question, "Why be moral?"

The quest for justification is answered by *theories* of morality. A moral theory is not just an attempt to explain the phenomenon of morality (as a theory in the natural or social sciences would). It is an attempt to justify morality, to provide the anchor for moral reasons. Using a different metaphor, many philosophers—especially Kant—would speak of "grounding" morality, building a rational foundation upon which all our reasons can then be combined in a single coherent structure. But, as we have earlier noted two different kinds of reasons and two different kinds of "anchors" or "groundings" so too we have two different kinds of theories of morality, corresponding to the two senses of justification. Morality may be justified by showing that it has its own moral terminus; the ultimate reason is itself moral, and this ultimate reason is more fundamental than any personal goals we might have, including happiness. Or, morality may be justified by showing that it leads, ultimately, to the attainment of these personal goals, such as happiness. But, in this latter case, moral reasons are not themselves the ultimate reasons. Morality is a means to something else, such as happiness.

Moral philosophers have traditionally given two rather formidable names to these two kinds of theories. Theories of morality which claim that morality provides its own ultimate anchor or grounding are called *deontological* (from the Greek word *deon,* or "duty"). Theories of morality which place some non-moral purpose at the end of moral reasoning are called *teleological* (from the Greek word *telos,* or "purpose"). We will examine several varieties of these theories in this final part of the book.

FACTS AND VALUES

The quest for justification brings us into the arena of "metaethics," in which we want to know not only what is good and what we ought to do but also what such terms as "good" and "ought" mean and whether our ethical claims are true or false, and how we know this. It is sometimes said, for example, that all statements of value are nothing but "expressions of personal feelings." If this were so, according to some ethicists (called, appropriately, "emotivists"), then ethical claims are neither true nor false (for feelings are neither true nor false), and the meaning of such critical terms as "good" and "ought" is nothing more than "I like this, and I want you to like it too." On the other hand, it has long been suggested that the word "good" ultimately means "good in God's eyes" and that "ought" means "God wills it." If we accept this analysis of "good" and "ought," then it is quite clear that there is an "objective" reference for our ethical claims. The statement "this is good" is true if God likes it; "you ought to do this" is true if God wills it. Ethical knowledge, in this analysis, would be knowledge of God. In the "emotivist" analysis, on the other hand, there can be no ethical knowledge, for ethical claims are neither true nor false but only expressions of personal, subjective feelings.

Metaethics, by clarifying what kind of terms such ethical words as "good" and "ought" are, sets the stage for justification of morality. If "good" refers to nothing but feelings, then it would seem (according to some authors) that the quest for justification is mistaken; at most, we can consider what sorts of feelings we regard as desirable and cultivate them through education and therapy. But if "good" refers to God's preferences, then the quest for justification is basically answered; morality is justified if it is God's will. There may be a problem to knowing exactly what it is that God wills, but at least we would know that morality, in general, is justified. The words "good" and "ought" have also been analyzed in such terms as "satisfying interests," "maximizing pleasure and minimizing pain," "producing happiness" and "promoting the good of society as a whole." In each case, the meaning of these critical terms implies the nature of justification for ethical claims; if "good" means "producing happiness" and "you ought to do x" means "doing x will produce the most happiness," morality in general can be justified by showing that its rules do, in fact, produce the most happiness.

This sensible schema for answering the quest for justification in terms of the analysis of "good" and "ought" hits a metaethical snag of monstrous proportions, however. There is a gap, philosophers have long argued, between value judgments and facts. It is true that we often justify moral claims by citing facts; "I claim that he has done wrong because he took money that he didn't earn," or "I was right to take the money because he said that he would give it to me." But there is always something less than entailment in such claims; one can add up the facts, but no value conclusion necessarily follows. I can point out that Harry always brings his wife flowers, never insults or strikes her, makes love to her tenderly, and he respects her career as well as makes a large salary himself. But none of this behavior entails the value judgment that "Harry is a good husband." Add as many more facts as you like about Harry and the logical outcome will be the same. No number of factual statements will let you deduce a value judgment.

David Hume, remarking on this logical problem, sums it up as "the impossibility of deriving an 'ought' from an 'is'." In this century, the same phenomenon has been characterized by Cambridge philosopher G. E. Moore in his

"Open Question Argument," namely, no matter how many facts you add together, the question is always open: "Yes, but is it GOOD?" Lists of facts do not yield values, and value judgments, in turn, can never be completely supported by the facts. No number of deeds determine that a person is virtuous, and no number of features make a thing good. Moore calls the attempt to define "good" in terms of facts the *naturalistic fallacy*. The alleged impossibility of justifying values by appeal to facts has troubled, if not devastated, ethics for most of this century. It has led to an awkward conclusion (for example, in David Hume and the modern "emotivists") that morality, and value judgments in general, cannot be justified. They can be derived from other value judgments, of course, but there is no factual anchor which can be used to justify them all. This means that there is something wrong with all those analyses which take the words "good" and "ought" to refer to some quality, such as God's will, or happiness, or social well-being. "This is good" is a value judgment; "People are happier now" is a statement of fact. But no number of statements of fact add up to, or entail, a value judgment. And that seems to mean that our quest for justification—at least in terms of some ultimate consideration which is not itself a value judgment—is impossible.

The hard division between facts and values, between "is" and "ought," is clasically argued in Hume's *Treatise of Human Nature*. He there complains that philosophers have traditionally neglected the distinction between judgments of fact and judgments of value. And indeed, the Greek philosophers, for example, would not have made much sense out of this distinction; they considered their ethical claims to be factually true. Saint Augustine, to take a very different example, would not have understood the worry that an ethical judgment might be the will of God but not thereby justified. But, Hume insists, it is one thing to know that a thing has a certain quality (e.g., that the fish has rotted or that Mr. Pickwick has an acute sense of humor), and something quite different to be repulsed or attracted to that thing because of that quality. So, too, virtue and vice are not the same as, and cannot be deduced from, such qualities as bravery, sharing one's fortune, and telling the truth. There is always the question, "But are these qualities desirable?" Facts never yield values; an "is" statement never entails an "ought":

> In every system of morality, which I have hitherto met with, . . . the author proceeds for some time in the ordinary way of reasoning . . . when all of a sudden I am surprised to find that, instead of the usual copulations of propositions *is* and *is not,* I meet with no proposition that is not connected with an *ought* or an *ought not*. This change is imperceptible; but it is, however, of the last consequence. For, as this *ought* or *ought not* expresses some new relation or affirmation, it is necessary that it should be observed and explained; and that at the same time a reason should be given, for what seems altogether inconceivable, how this new relation can be a deduction from others which are entirely different from it.
>
> (David Hume, *Treatise of Human Nature, p. 469)*

Hume's argument, re-dubbed the "naturalistic fallacy," is that no statement that something is good or bad, right or wrong, follows logically from a purely descriptive statement about what something is. Even the most extreme case—a description of the massacre of a defenseless village by bandits—does not yet warrant the conclusion that this slaughter is bad or wrong. (Imagine the same basic description supplied by a household exterminator, reporting to the homeowner on his treatment of a termite colony.) Psychologically, what must be added to the factual description to move us to repulsion is some evaluative concern on our part; logically, what must be added to the description is at least one premise that connects the "is" of description to the "ought" of morals, such as:

> factual premise: Three thousand creatures were killed.
> value premise: Killing is wrong.
> conclusion: Something wrong has been done.

Most moral philosophers have committed the "naturalistic fallacy," though few see it as a fallacy. We are all familiar with arguments such as the following (which are usually sufficiently complex so that the fallacy isn't so obvious):

> factual premise: The Bible says, "thou shalt not kill."
> value conclusion: Therefore, do not kill.

or:

> factual premise: People are basically selfish.
> value conclusion: Therefore, people ought to do what is in their own best

interests.

Sometimes, this "fallacy" is the core of an entire ethics, for example, in Aristotle and also in Kant. Aristotle begins with certain "facts" about human nature and deduces, in just the way forbidden by Hume, conclusions about what is good and right and what one ought to do. Kant begins with a factual premise about our rational faculties and similarly deduces that what we ought to do is to act rationally.

But is this "fallacy" really a fallacy? Or is Hume too strictly enforcing a dubious distinction? Could we save the traditional arguments by inferring an implicit premise, for example that we ought to do what is natural, thus undercutting the so-called naturalistic fallacy by introducing "nature" into the argument itself. Or, consider the following sequence of statements, formulated by the American philosopher John Searle as a counterexample to Hume's "is-ought" argument:

1 Jones uttered the words, "I hereby promise to pay you, Smith, five dollars."
2 Jones promised to pay Smith five dollars.
3 Jones placed himself under an obligation to pay Smith five dollars.

4 Jones is under an obligation to pay Smith five dollars.

5 Jones ought to pay Smith five dollars.

Searle claims that this sequence moves from purely factual statements to a conclusion that is clearly an "ought" type of judgment of value. How is this possible? Is there a concealed evaluative premise somewhere in the argument, for instance, the value judgment that one ought to keep one's promises? (Searle claims that this is merely a tautology—a purely trivial statement.) Are there implicit conditions (for example, our own cultural expectations and understanding of promises) which provide unspoken premises? Indeed, how many other such arguments can you formulate, in which the facts about certain institutions or established behavior seem to yield the clear "ought" type of value judgments? How defensible is Hume's "is-ought" distinction? And what does it imply about the general distinction between facts and values?

THE GOOD AND GOD'S WILL

The one fact which almost everyone agrees would have profound authority in moral matters and would justify morality beyond question is the existence of an all-knowing, all-powerful, just, and beneficent God. One might still raise the challenge of the "naturalistic fallacy," (or, in this case, it would be a "supernaturalistic fallacy"), but it would be hard to be convincing: that the commandments of the Supreme Being are just another set of facts, not yet a matter of what we ought to do. "Sure, God ordered us to do it, but is it indeed what we ought to do?" is not like, "Certainly it will give you pleasure, but that doesn't mean that it's good." One need not say that the words "good" and "ought" *mean* "commanded by God," but it is clear that the quest for justification would be solved if we could know that certain things are good and right *because* God commands them, whether or not the fact of God's existence logically entails the goodness of His commands.

One problem is that we don't seem to know, with any certainty or singularity, exactly what it is that God commands. The Bible is not a document written in a single voice; the Old and New Testaments depict God and His behavior quite differently and, consequently, they offer us different conceptions of morality. Even within the Old and New Testaments, there are a number of different viewpoints and, with them, somewhat different views of morality. At the risk of gross oversimplification, we might mention, for example, that the God of the Old Testament is sometimes introduced as a "Jealous" and at times a "Wrathful" God Who nevertheless watches over His "chosen people" and assures them victory in battle. Elsewhere in the Old Testament, God "tests" His people, allows their temples and their homeland to be destroyed and sometimes (as in the story of Job) subjects His people to excruciating torments. The God of the New Testament is celebrated rather as a "loving" God who is not so concerned with punishing us as with "saving" us through His own sacrifice. Even the Gospels give us significantly different portraits of Christ, which have given rise to very different interpretations of the meaning of God and Christianity as a whole.

The ethical visions that emerge from these conceptions of God differ accordingly: The Old Testament places its emphasis on obedience and God's Law. The New Testament, rather, takes as its highest commandment that we should *love* one another, which may be quite different from dutifully obeying the Law. It would be a mistake to suggest that these ethical views are incompatible (one can be loving and obedient at the same time), but it would also be a mistake to ignore the differences. Morality, as defined by God in the Bible, is not a singular set of commandments.

Nevertheless, it may be argued, there is sufficient agreement on the main matters of morality. There may be disagreements about the moral status of opening shops on the Sabbath and working mothers, but there is no disagreement about the prohibitions on murder, stealing, and adultery. There may be difficulties in using the Bible to provide definitions that answer every day-to-day question about our behavior, but there is no question about the fact that the Bible provides us with a general conception and justification of morality. Whether or not there are problems with particular applications of some universal commandments, the general nature of Judeo-Christian morality seems sufficiently clear.

Many people attempt to bypass problems of Biblical interpretation by appealing directly to the presence of God in themselves, "in the heart," or, more accurately, as faith and conscience. As religious feelings and promptings, such sensibility is unquestionable. But as ethics, as a source of moral commandments and justification, problems appear once again. How does one know that the promptings of one's "heart" or conscience are the Will of God? History is full of insane people who have felt such promptings acutely and had no doubts about their divine origin. Most likely, we know that the promptings of our "heart" or conscience are good because they conform to the morality taught in the Bible. (Thus we do not interpret the occasional urge to kill as a divine message, but we do so interpret the quiet urge to forgive someone.)

Even if one ignores questions of interpretation and accepts without question the idea that the Bible is the literal, revealed word of God, there are difficult questions confronting the most faithful reader. There are certain commandments and descriptions of the acts of God in the Bible—for example, God's order to Abraham to kill his son and His treatment of Job—which demand a justification. Family murder and wanton cruelty to the innocent are actions which we find morally intolerable; are they any more acceptable because God commands them? God on occasion wipes out entire populations by fire and/or flood, presumably including a number of innocent children at least. And even apart from these acts of Biblical vengeance, we can think of hundreds of "acts of God"—hurricanes, floods and earthquakes—in which the innocent have perished. What are we to make of this as ethics? Are God's actions and commands always moral?

Three answers have been most prevalent in the long history of this discussion.

- The first answer is that if God did or commanded these things, *therefore* they are good, without any qualification.
- The second answer is that these things, which seem to us to be very evil, are in fact good after all. (An appeal to "God's mysterious ways" or G. W. Leibniz's famous suggestion that this is, despite its problems, "the best of all possible worlds.")
- Third, one can insist that these acts are immoral and conclude that not everything that God does or commands is good.

(There is a fourth set of answers, of course, which is to insist that there is no God and, even if there were, He would make no difference to morality. We will not consider this set of answers here.)

The first answer is the straightforward acceptance of the thesis that God's will *defines* the Good, and if God does something out of line with what we call "morality," what He does is, nevertheless, good. This raises a problem, however, for, if one accepts these biblical accounts, one will conclude that God does not always insist on what we call "morality." One saves the view that what God wills is good but gives up the insistence that morality is what God always wills.

The second answer allows one to keep both the view that what God wills is good and the thesis that God justifies morality. The problem raised by the second answer is how to argue that God's biblical behavior can be understood as moral nevertheless. By appealing to "mysterious ways," one might save faith but thereby lose the direct and obvious connection between God and morality. We seem to require some independent conception of morality, such that we can then go on to show or believe that God's will is in accordance with it. The third and last answer accepts the conclusion that there is a difference between God and God's will and morality, but this means, in effect, we give up the idea that God alone can justify morality. We must have some independent conception and justification of morality, which may or may not apply to God as well. The third answer openly entails this view, where the second seems, rather, to be forced into it.

The conclusion that we have to know what is good independently of our belief in God goes back as far as Plato. In a dialogue called the *Euthyphro,* he considers the question whether something is good or right because God (the gods) commands it, or whether God (the gods) commands it because it is good or right. Socrates quickly convinces Euthyphro of the latter position, which means that what is good is good apart from the fact that God (the gods) wills it. Even if one is not troubled by the examples in the Bible, one can consider the following thought experiment: suppose someone were to uncover what seemed to be an authentic original manuscript from the Bible which gave us a perverse set of commandments, such as "Thou shalt kill," "Thou shalt steal," and "Thou shalt commit adultery as much as thou canst." Would we not reject the manuscript, its apparent authenticity aside, just because of our conviction that God would not command such immorality? But that means that we have a conception of morality which does not depend wholly on God's will; to the contrary, we are confident that God wills us to be moral because we believe that God Himself is a moral being.

The idea that God justifies morality need not mean that morality is justified because God wills it, however. It has often been suggested that God justifies morality because He *sanctions* it, that is, He sees to it that those who are moral are (eventually) rewarded and that those who are evil are (eventually) punished. This assurance is perfectly compatible with the idea that morality is quite independent of God's will. This view of God as sanction provides an excellent reason for being moral, namely, that one ought to be moral if one wants to avoid a dreadful punishment, and possibly gain a considerable reward as well.

The problem with this familiar viewpoint is that it confuses a purely selfish *motive* for being moral with the *justification* of morality. It makes morality a matter of *prudence,* which is precisely what the appeal to God as the justification of morality is intended to avoid. If morality is justified by appeal to God, it is because morality thereby becomes something more than an appeal to our own self-interests, namely, obedience to and love of an all-powerful, all-knowing, just, and beneficent Being. To confuse the prudential advantages of believing in God and being moral with the justification of morality by appeal to God's goodness is to undermine precisely this reason for turning to God in the first place.

One final point about God and the Good: there is at least one crucial virtue in Christian theology that is sometimes elevated "above morality." That virtue is *faith.* So long as faith is one of the cardinal virtues and is understood (as Kant, for example, understood it) as directed toward morality, there is no difficulty. But if faith in God is set apart and put "above" morality, belief in God may not serve as a justification of morality at all. The Danish philosopher Kierkegaard, for example, argues that this is the point of the Abraham and Isaac story in Genesis. Because he must prove his faith in God by committing the most immoral of acts, Abraham is forced to choose between faith and morality. The fact that God stops the sacrifice and gives the story a "happy ending" does not alter the fact that faith and morality can be opposed as well as conjoined.

TELEOLOGY AND HUMAN NATURE

A non-theological way to get around the gap between facts and values is to appeal morality to a peculiar kind of fact—the fact that something has a certain purpose. Thus one can say that the value of the heart in an animal is the fact that its purpose is to pump the blood around the body. This raises a further question, "What is the purpose of pumping the blood around the body?" But this too can be answered in terms of a purpose (to carry food and oxygen to the body, eliminate waste, etc.) Eventually, we will reach an answer citing the purpose, "to keep the creature alive," at which point we may want to know whether there is some purpose to this. A practical if not very sentimental answer might be, "Yes, we need pork from the pig as food in the fall, or "Yes, the cat has kittens which need her care." A more philosophical answer might be, "Because every living thing has its place in nature." But, especially when the creature in question is one of us, we have a sense of some further purpose, built into what we call "human nature," which, in addition to making life worth living, may also provide a justification for morality.

The philosophical term for such purposive explanations and justifications is *teleology.* The word comes from the Greek word for purpose, *telos.* Aristotle, most famously, gives a *teleological* justification of moral virtue in his *Nicomachean Ethics.* He argues the teleological position explicitly in the well-known opening sentence of that work: "Every art and every kind of inquiry, and likewise every act and purpose, seems to aim at some good; and so it has been well said that the good is that at which everything aims." In the case of human action, Aristotle argues, this ultimate good is "happiness" *(eudaimonia),* the life of virtuous action in accordance with reason. How does he come to this conclusion? It is essential to "human nature," he argues, to be rational; our purpose in life, therefore, is to be as rational as possible, and being so is, if successful, happiness.

A teleological justification of morality appeals the basic principles of morality or an account of the virtues to some overriding goal, built into human nature or nature in general. We have commented many times that Aristotle takes this ultimate goal to be "happiness," but we have not said that this goal is part of a much larger scheme of things in which Aristotle speculates upon the purpose of human existence and, ultimately, the purpose of the existence of the world. A teleological justification of morality, in other words,is a demonstration that our moral principles and virtues fit into some larger purpose. In the preceding section, we considered the possibility that our purpose in life might be a divine purpose, an expression of God's will. Jean-Paul Sartre's response to this might be worth noting: he insists that if there is no God, there is, therefore, no divine "design" which gives meaning to our lives. Expressing a similar view, the Russian novelist Fyodor Dostoevsky has one of his characters (Ivan Karamazov) declare, "If there is no God, everything is permitted." But the purpose of life does not have to come from God. Aristotle does not appeal to God in his theory of the "function," or *telos,* of human life, and one might well appeal to "nature's purpose" in support of human morality instead of any divine purpose. For example, some contemporary anthropologists and sociobiologists have suggested that we are by nature a cooperative species with built-in social instincts, a view propounded by Aristotle almost twenty-five hundred years ago when he defined "man" as a "social animal." And finally, in addition to God's purpose and nature's purpose, there are *our* purposes. If we could show, for example, that all human behavior is aimed at a single end, then that end might in turn serve as the justification of morality. Aristotle's suggestion that happiness is such an end has been repeated many times by many philosophers throughout history. Another prominent candidate has been pleasure, and the hedonist's thesis that all our actions ultimately aim at maximizing pleasure and minimizing pain can serve as a justification of morality (assuming, that is, that one can show that morality does indeed lead to maximum pleasure and minimum pain).

A third candidate for our ultimate purpose in life, which Aristotle conjoins with happiness, is reason. But reason as our *telos* raises certain difficult questions, since reason also provides the primary basis for a very different set of theories about morality, namely, *deontological* theories. Immanuel Kant, for example, offers a teleological argument (much like Aristotle's) to the effect that reason is our ultimate purpose in life and therefore we ought to be rational. But Kant then becomes the paragon deontologist and goes on to argue that morality is to be justified by appeal to reason itself, *not* by appeal to our purposes in life (our "inclinations," such as the desire to be happy). Nevertheless, it is essential to Kant's entire philosophy that reason is our ultimate purpose in life as well as the basis of morality. (The lesson here is that perhaps one should always be wary of broad philosophical distinctions; the great philosophers almost always transcend them.)

What about *our* purposes? Is there a single ultimate purpose to all our lives? Or, even if there is not a single purpose that is part of "human nature" as such, can we not still justify morality by appeal to the various purposes we pursue in life? We can do so as long as we are willing to be explicit about the *hypothetical* nature of such justifications. For example, if we want to be respected in our own communities, we might well defend the hypothetical imperative, "If you want to be respected, then be moral and virtuous." Indeed, most of our desires in life—which are not only conducted but made possible and meaningful in society—lend themselves to such hypothetical imperatives. One might accordingly argue that morality is a system of hypothetical imperatives, each of them conditional on some purpose or other that people pursue. Does this mean that all possible purposes require morality, that there is nothing that people might want which is better obtained by being immoral rather than moral? No, there will always be some people with purposes that dictate immorality. But they are far fewer than moral cynics have sometimes suggested, and, furthermore, it will be necessary for *our* purposes to thwart such people and their purposes. Such a qualified teleological view may therefore not provide the universal and absolute justification of morality sought by some philosophers, but it does supply a modest justification for most people. We can best get what we want out of life by being moral and virtuous. But this need not imply that morality is just a *means* to happiness. It may also be, as Aristotle insists, an essential *part* of happiness. In other words, one of our purposes in life is to be a "good person," and this goal already has morality built into it, not just as a means but as an end, perhaps even as the *telos* of what we consider best in "human nature."

ENLIGHTENED EGOISM

The suggestion that morality can be justified by showing that it is conducive to our purposes marks a shift away from a more impersonal justification of morality by appeal to some outside source, such as God or "human nature" in general, and toward a more personally oriented justification in terms of our personal aims and interests. At the end of this shift is that set of theories about morality which places all the burden of justification on the ability of morality to satisfy our individual interests. This set of theories typically goes by the name, *enlightened egoism.*

There are numerous variations. The most direct is:

1 Acting morally will always lead to the satisfaction of one's own interests.

This assumption would make life a lot easier, if it were true; we would never have to choose between what we want to do and what we ought to do. Unfortunately, the thesis is not very plausible, and life is accordingly not so simple.

2 Acting morally will usually lead to the satisfactions of one's own interests.

This thesis is certainly more plausible, and insofar as many of our interests include moral ambitions and are perfectly compatible with morality, it is safe enough. It does not do, however, what the enlightened egoist wants it to do: show that one is justified in pursuing one's own self-interest—even in those cases in which morality and self-interest seem to conflict.

3 Acting morally will usually, in the long run, lead to the satisfaction of more of one's interests than would be satisfied if one did not act morally.

Not surprisingly, the more one weakens the enlightened egoist's thesis, the more plausible it becomes. Nevertheless, this point would still be a hard one to prove to a very clever villain.

4 Acting morally will, overall, serve the greatest number of interests of the greatest number of people, including oneself.

We are now, however, beyond the range of egoism—enlightened or otherwise. It is one thing to claim that acting morally serves one's *own* interests; it is quite different to claim that acting morally serves a number of interests, including the interests of other people. This no-longer egoistic position is called "utilitarianism"; we will examine it in the following section.

5 Acting morally will, in addition to helping to satisfy some of one's own interests, set an example which will make the world a better place in which to live. Thus it will satisfy other interests that may not have been considered (such as encouraging friendliness in the streets, making everyone more supportive and dependable, and making life generally more enjoyable).

This version, unlike the others, is both egoist and edifying. It still appeals to one's own self interest, but in such a way that it obviously has appeal to most people's shared interests and concerns as well. Moreover, the causal thesis suggested here is probably true. The world would very likely be a more satisfying place if everyone were moral and virtuous. Unfortunately, many people would have to see this situation happen *before* they agreed to cooperate, and some people would inevitably find that, in a trusting, benign world, the profits of immorality would be even higher and the risks considerably lower. Such has been the undoing of many a pleasant society.

6 Acting morally, whether or not it results in the satisfaction of one's own interest, inspires feelings of self-righteousness and well-being which are their own satisfactions.

In other words, "goodness is its own reward." No doubt, but what if other rewards are more attractive? Does the feeling of righteousness suffice as a justification of morality, or is it, at best, one more motive—among many others—which makes being moral more attractive? It is a matter of common experience that self-righteousness can be extremely satisfying. But it is also a matter of common experience that many people find certain immoral satisfactions far more attractive.

There are other formulations, but these will do as representatives of position which is sometimes called "enlightened egoism." It is "egoism" insofar as the basis of one's concern, and also the basis of justification, is an appeal to one's own interests. It is "enlightened" insofar as it is not merely "selfish" but open to the suggestion that acting morally may serve one's own interests better. The problem with all such justifications, however, is that they tend to lose hold of the aim of a moral theory, which is to justify morality *apart* from appeal to purely personal interests. In other words, they tend at best to be prudential guidelines rather than justifications of morality as such. Morality, it is usually argued, always extends beyond the individual and his or her interests; the justification of morality, therefore, must go beyond personal interests too. What is even worse, however, is that such theories, even as prudential guidelines, tend to fail just when they are needed most—for example, when the reward for wrong-doing is huge and the threat of getting caught very small. One might well talk a chiseler out of a small sum by raising the prospect of going to prison, but one will hardly so influence the mobster who knows the enormous size of the stakes and the very remote chance of being caught.

UTILITARIANISM

The most influential theory of justification of morality, in the past several centuries, has been the theory called *utilitarianism*. It is at once a metaethical theory concerning the justification of morality and a formulation of the *summum bonum*—a single principle which will tell us how we ought to act. It is distinctively a teleological theory, emphasizing pleasure or happiness as the desired and desirable end of all human action. Morality is a means—a set of rules of thumb—about how to maximize happiness all around. The basic formulation of utilitarianism, accordingly, is "the greatest good for the greatest number," or what John Stuart Mill calls "the utility principle." It is a theory that is disinterested as well as based on self-interest (insofar as we consider everyone's happiness and not just our own). It is a theory about what is rational as well as what is right; it tells us both how to be happy and what we ought to do.

Utilitarianism begins with the view that what motivates us is first our own happiness, but it then derives the general objective principle that we ought therefore to act not just for our own happiness but for "the greatest good for the greatest number." It is a theory which tends to put much more emphasis on results than on principles and intentions, however. So obedience to the utility principle is not nearly so essential to the evaluation of actions and particular rules as the *consequences* of those actions and rules. (This has misled many people to define utilitarianism as any ethical theory that worries only about consequences ["consequentialism"], but this focus is not its defining characteristic.) Utilitarianism is essentially a teleological theory which emphasizes pleasure or happiness as the ultimate end of action. It is not at all blind or indifferent to intentions or rules, but the emphasis is on beneficial and harmful results rather than on a Kantian "good will," which however good may nonetheless make everyone miserable.

Utilitarianism, in one sense, goes back to the beginning of ethics (thus prompting Mill to proclaim that it has been presupposed by every moral philosopher). In the very broad sense that Mill has in mind, utilitarianism is no more than the generally acceptable and minimal view that morality requires that other people's interests must be taken into account, and everyone has an interest in being happy. But, in its more specific versions, utilitarianism is an ethical theory that promises an unusually precise means of calculating what is right and what is wrong. That promise is, indeed, one of the theory's main attractions. Utilitarianism, properly formulated, will not only show us how morality is to be justified; it will also show us, in detail, exactly what morality is, and what, in every circumstance, we ought to do. The notion of utility can be converted into discrete quantities of pleasure and pain, which can be measured and compared. We must add to this the second basic principle of utilitarianism, "the principle of justice" which requires that "each person counts for one and no more than one." In other words, everyone's pleasure (and pain) is to count equally, and it is the overall amount of pleasure (and pain) that determines what one ought to do.

Utilitarianism had its origins in the Enlightenment, but the founder of the utilitarian movement proper was an English reformer named Jeremy Bentham, who developed a "happiness calculus" to evaluate every action. For every decision, one would add up all the various pleasures it might bring to everyone concerned and subtract the amount of pain. One would compare that total with the amount resulting from alternative courses of action, and one would choose that course of action which maximized pleasure and minimized pain. Bentham's immediate aim was to reform the hopelessly complex and sometimes cruel English legal system by developing a schedule of punishments which would just outweigh the pleasure of the wrongful act, thus minimizing the amount of pain to the smallest degree necessary to deter crime. But the theory also has general application as an overall ethical theory.

Suppose, for example, your elderly grandparents have asked you to come home for Thanksgiving dinner. Unfortunately, however, you have an extremely important and difficult examination on the following Monday, not to mention that some of your friends, who are staying in town, are planning a great party for that Saturday night. Your parents (who know about the exam but not the party) advise you, unhelpfully, "Do what you think best, dear," but you know that they would like to see you with your grandparents. Now, the standard moral evaluation of this situation would ask such questions as "What is your duty in this case?" or "Do you have an obligation to your grandparents?" Not the utilitarian. The question is, rather, which course of action—going home or staying in town—will maximize happiness? You cannot, of course, count your own happiness as more important than that of your parents or grandparents, or, though they are less involved, that of your friends. Your own happiness does count, however, and presumably that will be the first calculation: Which course of action will give you more pleasure and less pain? In the short term, studying is unpleasant (give it a minus 3) but the party will be terrific (plus 6). The trip home is a bit of a hassle (minus 2) but you do like your grandparents (plus 3). You saw your parents two weeks ago, so you don't expect any particular pleasure or pain there, but you do enjoy driving your father's new Grand Prix (plus 2). Longer-term, if you do badly in the exam you may make it hard for yourself for years (minus 12), but if your elderly grandparents should die without your seeing them, you will also feel guilty for years (minus 12). Doing well on the exam will have considerable advantages for the future (plus 12). On the other hand, the feeling of righteousness at having pleased both your parents and your grandparents will be considerable and durable (plus 4). As for your parents, grandparents, and friends, those calculations are rather simple: your grand-parents will be delighted to see you (plus 6) and your parents will too (plus 3). If they don't see you, they will be disappointed (minus 3, minus 1). Your friends (you hope) would love you to come to the party (plus 1) but probably won't even notice if you don't (zero). (The complex role of self-esteem and wishful thinking is difficult to calculate here.) But now, according to Bentham, we are in a position to make a completely rational decision without bringing in such obscure and unmeasurable concepts as "duty" or "obligation." Our cal-culation looks like this:

Go home	Stay and study
-2	-3
$+3$	$+6$
$+2$	-12
-12	$+12$
$+4$	-3
$+6$	-1
$+3$	
0	$+1$
Totals:	
$+4$	0

The answer, clearly, is that you should go home for Thanksgiving.

There are complications not included here, in addition to the difficulties in calculating people's feelings (including one's own). Suppose, though you couldn't have easily predicted such an outcome beforehand, your friends' party got out of hand. The police arrived and arrested several people. (You probably would have been one of them.) That, needless to say, would considerably add to the deficit side of staying i town and going to the party. (In this case, it would not have changed the final outcome.) And you forgot to include in the calculation the fact that you and your father have been having a continuing argument about your buying a car, which will put quite a damper on your rapport with your parents and cancel your Grand Prix driving privileges (minus 3, cancel plus 2).

These possibilities add a difficult question: To what extent must the utili-tarian calculation take into account all the possible consequences of an action? To the extent we are concerned with the *actual* consequences, it would seem that *all* consequences, no matter how unforeseen or unpredictable, count equally in the calculation of goodness and badness. To the extent that we are concerned just with *envisioned* consequences, on the other hand, we are, rather, concerned with what a responsible person could reasonably expect to happen. One must add into the calculus, however, the effort, pleasure, and (more often) pain that go into the calculation itself. For example, if you spend the two weeks before Thanksgiving worrying about what to do, not studying, and being irritable with your friends and (on the phone) with your parents, you may well cause yourself and everyone else sufficient pain to cancel out all the calculations you are trying so rationally to make. Indeed, in many if not most of our decisions in life, trying too hard to make a precisely rational decision is itself quite irrational.

The ultimate champion of utilitarianism was not Bentham but John Stuart Mill, the son of Bentham's colleague, James Mill. But philosophers are famous for their disagreement, and disagreements within agreed-upon viewpoints are often more drastic than disagreements between viewpoints (when theorists often simply refuse to talk to one another). In his definitive pamphlet *Utilitarianism* (1861), Mill defends the principle of utility as the only intelligible basis for ethics, but at the same time he amends Bentham's calculus of sheer *quantity* of pleasure with a conception of the *quality* of pleasure. Thus, "it is better to be a Socrates dissatisfied, than a pig satisfied," Mill writes. But this amendment all but destroyed the simplicity of Bentham's calculus, for, after all, it was the ability to calculate all ethical decisions on a single scale of pleasure and pain that made the utilitarian program so attractive. Finally, Mill maintains, all disagreements could be settled on a single basis, since all of us, everywhere, are concerned with our own pleasure and pain as an ultimate goal. But as soon as we add this second dimension, that simplicity disappears. It is clear what Mill is concerned about. Suppose one gets much more pleasure in drinking beer than reading Shakespeare. Mill does not want to be forced to conclude that the first act is better than the second. But, once one has shifted the argument away from measurable quantities of pleasure and pain (even assuming that these are available), how does one evaluate their qualities? We have lost our calculus, and it is by no means clear that any more complicated "qualitative" calculus could take its place.

"The greatest good for the greatest number": it sounds like a simple, singular theory. It is not, as we can see from this disagreement between Bentham and Mill (on quantity versus quality of pleasure). Indeed, recent theorists have distinguished a surprisingly large number of utilitarian theories, all of them within the "greatest good for the greatest number" idea, but yet significantly different. For example, utilitarianism is sometimes interpreted as a retrospective way of evaluating the actual consequences of actions; sometimes it is interpreted as a technique for planning actions and, accordingly, evaluating intentions rather than consequences (assuming, of course, that good intentions also take into account the probable consequences).

Mill himself incorporates both these views, adding that the first is a means of evaluating actions and the second a means of evaluating personal character. Utilitarians are also split on whether or not to accept Mill's and Bentham's too-easy equation of happiness and pleasure. Like Aristotle, many utilitarians want to separate the two and insist that it is happiness that is important, not pleasure as such (though obviously one wouldn't want to suggest that the two are opposed). But "happiness," as we have seen, is a broad and equivocal concept, while pleasure and pain at least seem to be precise. Thus more orthodox utilitarians have continued the emphasis on quantifiable (if not qualifiable) pleasure as a way of saving the "utility" of utilitarianism. Other authors have rejected these central ends altogether, preferring to speak only in the most noncommittal terms of "good and evil consequences," thus sacrificing the very precision that Bentham and Mill thought essential to utilitarianism. What remains constant in all versions, of course, is the emphasis on desirable consequences, "the greatest good for the greatest number." But, despite its apparent simplicity, utilitarianism is not a single theory but many, with very different emphases and, appropriately, many different consequences.

Perhaps the most important division among utilitarians today turns on a question we have not yet broached, namely, is it an *individual* action to which we apply the utilitarian calculus, or is it, rather, a *class* of actions? Suppose, for example, I am tempted to tell a lie. This is, of course, one of the standard moral dilemmas, in which the principle of utility is typically thought to be inappropriate. ("It doesn't matter that everyone will be happier if you lie; it's *wrong* to tell a lie!") It is easy to imagine an instance in which the happy consequences of a lie overwhelm the few painful consequences, including the modicum of shame or guilt and the small effort necessary for the cover-up. Furthermore, the consequences of telling the truth would be devastating for the person to whom the upsetting truth is told and, consequently, extremely unpleasant for the truth-teller too. Looking only at this individual act, the utilitarian decision is obvious: One ought to lie, thereby maximizing happiness and minimizing suffering. But, a critic might well contend, it is never an isolated action that is the subject of our deliberations and our ethics; to call an act a "lie" is already to place it in a class of actions which are morally dubious. When we evaluate the consequences of lying, therefore, it is not just a question of whether *this* lie has good or bad consequences for everyone involved. It is a question of whether *lying* as such has good or bad consequences.

This point changes the view of the matter considerably, needless to say. An individual act of lying may well have obviously good consequences, but it is not at all clear that lying *in general* has anything but bad consequences. Lying makes both liars and those lied to unhappy in a myriad of ways, and the "happy" or "white" lie is something of an exception. (Some theorists would even insist that it is not a lie at all.) Thus we can distinguish two distinct forms of utilitarianism (both of which, by the way, seem to be contained in Mill's *Utilitarianism*):

1 Always do that act which will bring the greatest good to the greatest number (*act*-utilitarianism).

2 Always do that *kind* of act (or follow that rule) which will bring the greatest good to the greatest number (*rule*-utilitarianism).

Why have utilitarians split on this seemingly technical issue? (Mill, by contrast, seems content to consider the general implications of an action as part of its consequences; in other words, implicit support for a rule or a class of actions is one of the considerations in deciding the utilitarian "quality" of an act.) The reason is that as act-utilitarianism has been increasingly challenged by difficult cases, rule-utilitarianism has provided a way to save utilitarianism in general from the most troublesome objections. For example, the objection has often been raised that a proper calculation of the consequences of an action is humanly impossible (thus our concern for unforeseen consequences and the difficulty of predicting people's feelings in our Thanksgiving example). But, in rule-utilitarianism, one need not undertake such individual calculations, for they have already been provided in the general form of a rule. Thus, "Lying is wrong" is a summary statement of centuries of research and observation: Lying in general leads to bad consequences.

A second much-noted difficulty may be summarized in the following example: Suppose we were to carry out the utilitarian calculations appropriate to two courses of action, one of which includes both a lie and a clearly unfair action in which another person will be cheated. (Consider, for example, selling a used car and claiming that it is in "excellent running condition," not mentioning that you know that it will fall apart in five miles.) Suppose, too, that the balance of utility in your calculation comes out even. (Suppose that the person buying the car is quite rich and has several other cars, while you desperately need the money and have to leave town soon.) On a strict act-utilitarian basis, the choice between the two is indifferent. Or, if the cheating and lying side emerges a few utility points ahead, you will follow that course of action as the "better" one.

Not surprisingly, these conclusions are considered to be intolerable by most people; the choice to lie and cheat or not to should never be a matter of indifference, and lying and cheating are not "better" just because the utility is slightly greater by doing so. One could, as a convinced act-utilitarian, dig in one's heels and insist that such moral concerns are indeed irrelevant and one *should* make decisions only on a strict act-utilitarian basis. But most utilitarians regard such examples as more than sufficient to damage the act-utilitarian theory, and prefer to modify utilitarianism to get around them. Rule-utilitarianism is the best known of these modifications.

The various forms of utilitarianism—all of them originating in the simple, appealing "principle of utility" formulated by Bentham and Mill—reflect the problems in the theory; each variation is an attempt to modify the theory to answer an objection. (The strength and influence of utilitarianism are exemplified by the number of serious revisions of it. Less compelling theories are usually just left to wither away.) The first variation of the theory was Mill's objection to Bentham's purely quantitative theory, which placed too much emphasis on material pleasures and not enough on the harder-to-quantify pleasures of the mind and spirit—the arts, friendship, philosophy. A more recent variation in utilitarian theory is the formulation of rule utilitarianism—in contrast to act-utilitarianism—as a way of meeting the objection that clearly wrong acts might, in a single instance, be shown to maximize pleasure and minimize pain for everyone involved. Rule-utilitarianism blocks this possibility by insisting that a class of actions, not just a single instance, improves the general well-being. It also accounts for the value of moral rules.

Utilitarianism continues to be one of the most thoroughly discussed ethical theories and strategies of moral justification, but it is not without its continuing problems. As a theory of "utility," it has always been accused of being "vulgar" and devoid of more spiritual awareness, despite Mill's efforts to add "quality" to it. Indeed, Mill counters this objection even in *Utilitarianism,* when he answers religious critics who attack him for appealing morality to a business-like calculation of pleasures instead of to God or the Scriptures. Mill's reply is simply that God, being good, wanted us to be happy, and so God Himself is a utilitarian and utilitarianism is just a precise way of interpreting God's will.

A more telling set of objections is aimed at the utilitarian emphasis on *consequences* (whether of an action or a class of actions, whether actual consequences or intended consequences). When a moral principle is presented absolutely (as in the Ten Commandments, for example), it is accepted first, and the question of consequences does not arise, or arises only afterward. (Moses did not ask Jehovah, "But what's so bad about people coveting their neighbor's ox?") Such rules may admit of qualifications and exceptions, but their status as rules comes first. We may object to this emphasis on rules, and we may use utilitarianism (even rule-utilitarianism) against it. But we cannot simply deny that insofar as utilitarianism is supposed to be a theory of the justification of morality, it puts its priorities suspiciously backward, deriving (or rejecting) rules on the basis of their consequences, rather than evaluating consequences in the light of the rules. Thus, some critics of utilitarianism insist that it is intolerably anarchistic, allowing for no essential social structures—in other words, no ethos—apart from the contingencies of utility.

Three further objections have been leveled against all of the various forms of utilitarianism:

1 Different kinds of consequences may be extremely difficult to compare. Throughout our discussion, we have assumed the intelligibility of Bentham's first premise, that different units of "utility" (whether pleasure and pain, happiness and unhappiness, or good and evil) can be placed on a similar scale and weighed. Mill is already suspicious of this, which is why he introduces the notion of "quality" of pleasure, allowing for different scales of measurement but thereby also destroying the simplicity and singularity of Bentham's calculus. But whether it is act- or rule-utilitarianism that concerns us, and whether actual or intended consequences of different courses of action are involved, is it at all clear that we can compare different values on anything like a similar set of scales? For example, suppose a city has a financial crisis and one of the suggestions for saving money is closing down the art museum and selling its contents. Closing down the museum may save the taxpayers thousands of dollars, but what is the cultural "cost" of doing so? Indeed, to speak of "cost" in this case already betrays one of the hidden assumptions of utilitarianism—that value in general can be placed on a general scale of *exchange,* with a single unit of exchange, namely, money. This may indeed be a valid assumption when we are wondering how many chickens we should sell in order to be able to buy a new barn. But when the less tangible aspects of human life are involved, we are rightfully squeamish about even trying to put a dollar value on them. There is something ethically discomforting about life insurance, however practically necessary such protection may be. There is something unsettling about buying and selling people's time and dignity in jobs that are a waste of time or just plain foolish. There is something unnerving about the art market and commercialized religion, not because money, art, and religion don't mix (gods have always demanded material sacrifices, for example), but because the values of art and religion—like our lives, time, and dignity—do not seem reducible to an exchange rate in dollar amounts. But even if we delete the financial currency of exchange implicit in the utilitarian formula, it would still seem "vulgar"— to use the insult Nietzsche used against Mill and his followers—to consider all pleasures and pains, all kinds of happiness and unhappiness, in the same scheme of things, even if qualified by an insistence on "quality."

2 The consequences of an act or a class of actions may be clearly positive and, nevertheless, the act is just as clearly wrong. Against act-utilitarianism, we have already considered the case of a single action (selling a decrepit used car and lying about it) in which the marginal utility of a "better" sale does not compensate for the lying and cheating that are employed to make that sale. But one might show that such examples are also true of an entire class of actions and thus operate against rule-utilitarianism as well. Suppose, for example, it could be demonstrated that adultery would save more marriages than it would destroy and would make people more happy than miserable. Would adultery then be a moral act? Such research has often been attempted, but the results have been generally rejected, not because of lack of evidence but because of apparent ethical irrelevance. If adultery is wrong, as most people still believe, it does not matter whether it is conducive to happiness or not.

3 The most definitive objection to utilitarianism aims at the principle of utility itself. Mill protects the principle from abuse (for example, criticizing a very powerful man who makes himself happy at everyone else's expense) by insisting that "everyone counts for one and only one." The rule-utilitarian protects the theory against a gleeful sadist, for example, by insisting that it is not a single instance that is in question but a kind of action, namely, sadism. But even within this principle of equality and with the rule-utilitarian proviso, a serious ambiguity remains. Suppose a majority of the citizens of a town pass a tax law which, in effect, takes $500 from every member of a minority and, at the same time, cuts taxes by the same amount (the deficit coming from the education budget, no doubt) for every member of the majority. Suppose, too, the majority members proudly announce their solution to the civic budget problem to financially pressed cities all over the nation, as a general means of balancing budgets. Leaving aside the difficulty of measuring amounts of pleasure and pain merely on the basis of dollar amounts, it seems clear that this act (and this type of act) is not wrong according to utilitarianism because it maintains utility and makes more people happy. And yet, we would probably all agree, the act is clearly unjust. Even good consequences do not compensate for injustice.

A second, more sadistic, example favored by many critics of utilitarianism is this: Suppose that a rather sick society gets great joy out of the spectacle of a few innocent people being tortured to death. (Consider Rome during some of its darker days, for example.) On the utilitarian account, the great joy of the spectators—if it outweighs the suffering of the few victims—is sufficient to make their behavior moral. Indeed, given a sufficiently large component of sadism in a population, this means of maximizing pleasure—if not minimizing pain—might be promoted as a national sport. (Boxing? Pro-football?) But this, we object, would surely be unfair and immoral. This example, like the last one, shows that utilitarianism cannot take proper account of *justice.*. The well-being of the majority is one thing, but justice may be something else. Happily, the two are usually commensurate. But, nevertheless, as an overall theory of the justification of morality, utilitarianism has been accused of failing a crucial test; it cannot provide adequate justification for some of our most important moral convictions. We should end by noting that all these objections have been answered by various utilitarians but, despite their arguments, many philosophers have been persuaded to look elsewhere for the justification of morality.

KANT AND DEONTOLOGY

It is in reaction to the objections to utilitarianism—particularly its apparent inadequacy in accounting for justice—that a great many philosophers have turned to an older tradition in which moral principles are not conditional on consequences or mere means to happiness, but absolute. The origins of this theory, of course, go back to the beginning of human history, when the word of the chief, or the king, or God, was given unconditionally and without invitation to appeal on the basis of consequences. Whereas utilitarian theories ground morality in the pursuit of human happiness, these theories ground morality in the concept of *duty.* We noted that such theories are *deontological* theories, from the Greek root *deon,* meaning "duty." In deontological theories, an act or a class of actions is justified by showing that it is *right,* not by showing that it has good consequences (though, again, it is usually assumed that both will be the case).

The foremost modern defender of a deontological theory is Immanuel Kant. He was reacting to the early "utility" theories of Hume and other Enlightenment philosophers, and he anticipated the later objections to utilitarianism (Kant wrote seventy years before Mill) by insisting that what makes an act right or wrong cannot be its consequences—which are often entirely out of our hands and a matter of luck—but the *principle* (or "maxim") which guides the action. "Nothing ... can be called good without qualification, except a *good will,*" he writes at the beginning of his *Groundwork of the Metaphysic of Morals.* And having a "good will" means acting with the right intentions, according to the right maxims or principles, doing one's duty *for its own sake* rather than for personal gain or out of what Kant calls "inclination" (desires, emotions, moods, whim, inspiration, or sympathy). This is the heart of Kant's ethics, "duty for duty's sake," not for the sake of the consequences, whether one's own good or "the greatest good for the greatest number."

What is the court of appeal for deontological theories of justification? The utilitarian, like the "enlightened" egoist and the Aristotelean teleologist, could appeal to actual human desires and aspirations. But the deontological theory, as "unconditional" or "absolute," rejects just those desires and aspirations as the ultimate court of appeal (though, for Kant and almost all other deontologists, they nevertheless remain important). The court of appeal of a deontological theory is duty, and this means, an appeal to *authority.* But this does not necessarily mean that the deontologist gives up moral responsibility and passes it on to God or those in power. Some deontologists, of course, do appeal morality to the authority of God (thus the justification of morality by appeal to God's will has the earmarks of *both* a teleological and a deontological theory; it refers to purposes [God's purpose], but it is also an absolute appeal to His authority). Other deontologists appeal to the Law ("It doesn't matter what you think; it's the Law"). But at least one leading deontologist believes that the appeal to authority necessary to justify morality is also an appeal to one's own moral *autonomy* in deciding what is right and what is wrong. That deontologist is Kant, and his theory continues to be one of the two basic starting points of most modern ethical theories (the other being utilitarianism).

On Kant's theory, the ultimate court of appeal for the justification of morality is the court of *reason,* or what he calls *pure practical reason.* Each of us is *rational;* that is, each of us has the ability to reason and arrive at the *right* way to act, by ourselves and without appeal to any "outside" authority. This ability to reason and decide for ourselves is what Kant calls "autonomy" (as opposed to "heteronomy"). To justify morality, therefore, is to show that it is rational, and to justify any particular moral principle is to show that it is in accordance with the principles of reason. Morality, we have already said, is characterized by Kant as a system of *categorical imperatives,* that is, commands which are unconditional. We can now appreciate better what this means; they are unconditional, not only in the sense that they apply to everyone without deferring to personal interests, but also in the sense that they apply without regard to consequences of any kind. They are principles of reason and, as such, are not bound to the contingencies of life. Here we can see a positive use of the infamous gap between values and facts; Kant takes this to be the heart of reason— that it envisions the world according to its own ideals and is not determined merely by the facts of the world.

Because moral principles are rational principles, according to Kant, their justification must be a purely *formal* (or *logical*) justification. To prove that an act is immoral, it is not enough to show that its actual or probable consequences would be disastrous; one must demonstrate that its principle itself is "contradictory" and impossible. One of Kant's examples will serve as an illustration of what this means: Suppose I am considering borrowing money from you under false pretenses, by lying and telling you that I will pay you back next week (when in fact I will be in Hawaii, never to return). Now the utilitarian would ask for the consequences (whether of the act or of a kind of act); Kant asks for more. What if, he argues, I were to apply the "maxim" of my act (that is, the principle upon which I am acting) to everyone else, and urge them to act similarly? Since morality is essentially a product of reason, I *must* be able to do this, for I cannot apply principles to myself alone. (The utilitarian would agree with this.) What would be the result? It would be to undercut the whole practice of promising to repay borrowed money, and if anyone were to ask, "Can I borrow some money and pay you back next week?" everyone would simply laugh, for such words would have become meaningless. Thus, Kant points out, the maxim "contradicts" itself. This is not just to say that the consequences of generalizing the maxim would be disastrous. (A rule-utilitarian would agree with that.) It is a formal or logical inadequacy: the universalization of the maxim makes the action in question incomprehensible. What would count as lying, in a community in which no one could ever be expected to tell the truth?

What motivates Kant's deontology is a firm conviction that morality is something more than the customs and ethos of a particular society, something more than a set of sympathetic feelings we experience toward other people and other creatures. He believes—and wants to prove—that morality is the same everywhere, built into the structure of the human mind just as the basic categories of truth and knowledge are. This is not to say that everyone everywhere in fact accepts all the same moral principles, of course; neither do all people accept the principles of modern science (which Kant also insists are universal and necessarily true "for every rational being"). Every human being has the *faculty* of rationality, but not every human being actually cultivates and realizes that faculty. In effect, what Kant wants to do with his philosophy (as Aristotle wanted to do with his) is to help people cultivate their rational faculty by understanding better what it means to be moral and consequently being more moral. But he will readily admit that most people and most of the peoples of the world fall far short of his rational ideal.

The crucial point in Kant is his view that it is not just our personal "inclinations" that motivate us to act. There is a far nobler source of motivation, and that is reason itself. In other words, Kant thinks that egoism, enlightened or otherwise, is just plain false. We are not motivated only by self-interest; we are also motivated to act for the sake of reason alone. Thus the recognition that we have a duty need not be further supported by some realization of self-interest; it is enough that we recognize our duty, and therefore want to do it. It is this sense of motivation, not of sympathy or any other inclination but of "the moral law within," that makes Kant's ethics the most powerful defense of "pure" morality in the history of the subject.

This emphasis on "the moral law within" and the notion of autonomy is utterly at odds with the grounding of morality in "utility" or any other social concept. For Kant, morality is essentially an individual—and a universal—affair. It is individual in that, as an autonomous subject, everyone has both the ability and the duty to reason and figure out what is right. It is universal in that, although each of us is autonomous, the laws of reason and the principles of morality dictated by reason are necessary and shared in common by all of us. But what is left out of this polarity is the social fabric of an ethos, the sense of our being "social animals," as Aristotle defined us so long ago. This is not to say, of course, that Kant does not have a keen sense of community and the need for all of us to get along together. Indeed, one of his "formulations" of the categorical imperative is that we should always act as if we were members of the perfect community, which he calls "the kingdom of ends." But it is doing our duty itself that is essential to morality; the good society, it is hoped, will follow. Kant is well aware that societies as well as individuals can be immoral. But morals, therefore, cannot consist of the values and relationships within a society. There is also reason, which transcends all societies and imposes upon them a set of rational principles of duty which are to be obeyed by all.

Deontological theories such as Kant's succeed precisely where utilitarian theories fail—in showing how moral principles are unconditional and not dependent on utility, especially in those cases where the greatest good for the greatest number can be realized through injustice or cruelty. Put in a different way, what Kant and the deontologists show is that individuals have *rights*—and other people have corresponding duties to respect those rights. It is not enough to show that society would be better served if one or two unfortunate but innocent individuals were put to death or tortured for the amusement of everyone else. Nor will it do for a society to benefit the majority at the expense of injustice to the minority, for there are moral claims which have authority even where the greater happiness is not served.

Where the deontologist runs into trouble, accordingly, is just where the utilitarian succeeds. We noted that one of the great attractions of utilitarianism is its emphasis on human happiness and well-being. The deontologist cannot be indifferent to such concerns, but, nevertheless, they clearly play a secondary role in the theory of morality. In one sense, we can understand the reason for this: Morality must be grounded independently of personal inclinations (including the desire to be happy), for the inclinations are (1) variable and undependable; therefore, (2) not necessary and universal; and (3) a matter of "nature" rather than of free and rational will. But is it possible or tolerable that happiness should be opposed to morality? If morality means doing our duty, and duty is independent of what is in our own self-interest, could it be that the morally good person should be oblivious to happiness, and perhaps very unhappy besides? Kant rejects this conclusion, insisting that we even have a duty to be happy. His odd reason is that an unhappy person is not in an optimum mood to carry out a duty. Furthermore, he says, rationality dictates that it would be most unreasonable to expect us to do our duty if there were no justice, no commensuration of good and happiness, no punishment for evil. But, though it is obvious that we do not always find such justice in this world, Kant argues that its absence should lead us to conclude that there must be justice elsewhere, in an afterlife, judged by an all-knowing and all-powerful beneficent God. Thus Kant, like many deontologists before him, ultimately appeals his strict sense of morality and duty to religion, albeit a "rational" religion, one to be defended "through reason alone."

Deontological theories of ethics are still very much at the forefront of the subject. Professor John Rawls at Harvard, who is perhaps the most important moral philosopher in the United States today, has developed a deontological theory with many affinities to Kant, in particular its emphasis on universal principles and the centrality of rights. Rawls's theory is concerned not so much with individual moral decisions, however, but, rather, with the social dimension of justice. In his book *A Theory of Justice,* he defends two basic principles:

1 The equality principle: "Each person engaged in an institution or affected by it has an equal right to the most extensive liberty compatible with a like liberty for all."

2 The difference principle: "Inequalities as defined by the institutional structure or fostered by it are arbitrary unless it is reasonable to expect that they will work out to everyone's advantage and provided that the positions and offices to which they attach or from which they may be gained are open to all."

The second principle clearly refers to utilitarian considerations, but it is, nevertheless, a principle of reason. What it does—and what utilitarianism does not do—is to specify the kinds of advantages and disadvantages that can be justified. In Rawls's view, inequities are inevitable in society, but there is a rational way of justifying them. An inequality must benefit everyone, not only the person who has a special advantage but, especially, people who are the least advantaged. Thus it can be argued that it is fair to allow some people to make fortunes from investments because, even if their doing so makes them much wealthier than everyone else, it also supports industry and improves the quality of life for everyone.

Rawls introduces his deontological theory in a particularly dramatic way. In Part Three of this book, we mentioned the "social contract" theory, in which all members of a society are said to agree to the terms of a general contract, according to which they have rights and duties as citizens. Rawls begins his theory by asking us to imagine that we are in "the original position" of having to set up a society, with inevitable advantages for some people and disadvantages for others. The complication is that none of us knows what particular position we will have in society. What is the rational thing to do in such a situation? It is to design a society that is as equal as possible, in which everyone has the best chance possible and in which those who are most disadvantaged will benefit from the society too. For example, we might well decide to give some people more power than others in order to form a government, on the ground that everyone will benefit from an orderly society, whereas almost everyone would suffer in a society where there was equality but universal chaos. A familiar domestic example of Rawls's "difference principle" is the case in which the oldest child in a group is asked to cut an apple pie for all the children. (He or she will have last choice of the pieces.) It is clearly rational in such an instance to cut the pieces as equally as possible or, if this is impossible, to make the smaller slices as large as possible. So, too, in a just society, there will be as much equality as possible, not just as a matter of increasing the general welfare but as a matter of reason—a matter of justice.

EXISTENTIALISM, EMOTIVISM, AND MOORE

In the preceding sections, we have discussed two general strategies for justifying morality: teleological theories (including utilitarianism) which appeal to the ultimate purposes and consequences of moral behavior, and deontological theories which appeal, rather, to the authority (especially rational authority) of moral principles. We have also considered a number of particular courts of appeal, among them God's will, practical reason, the formal consistency of principles, the "design" of nature and human desires and aspirations, including "selfishness" as well as more "enlightened" egoism. For more than two thousand years, debate has been waged over these strategies and the ultimate validity of these appeals, and ethicists will probably continue debating their various advantages and inadequacies for the next two thousand years as well. But there is a different kind of possibility, and that is that the entire enterprise of justifying morality is a mistake. Perhaps morality cannot be justified, or perhaps to try to justify morality already demonstrates something seriously wrong with morality, such that we are not convinced of its necessity without some "proof" or "demonstration."

This doubt can be found even in the best defenders of morality. Some of the Sophists who are Socrates's interlocutors in Plato's dialogues offer persuasive arguments—that "might makes right," that justice is nothing but timid self-ishness, that "man is the measure of all things"—and it is not entirely clear that Socrates refutes them. Aristotle warns us at the beginning of his *Ethics* that we should not expect more precision or proof than the subject allows and insists that there is no point in trying to convince people of the importance of the virtues if they have not already been brought up correctly to accept and practice them. Mill prefaces his "proof" of utilitarianism with the similar warning that one cannot really "prove" ultimate principles in ethics.

Some authors in ethics, however, have embraced the skeptical idea that one may not be able to justify morality, without apology or hesitation. David Hume, most notably, rejects the possibility of justifying morals in any impor-tant sense (just as he rejects the possibility of justifying our knowledge of the world). Reason, in particular, cannot justify morality, and though morals are based on our "sentiments," according to Hume, this hardly counts as "justifi-cation" in the strong sense demanded by philosophers. After all, if our senti-ments were entirely different, so would be our morals; the question of which morals are "right" thus seems beside the point. It just happens that we are endowed by nature with certain sentiments (as it happens that we are endowed by nature with certain facilities for knowledge), and that's the end of it.

But that is not the end of the argument for the more radical critics of the traditional emphasis on justification. Friedrich Nietzsche accepts many of the same arguments advanced by Hume but adds some devastating arguments of his own. He asks, Why the emphasis on justification, if not that morality itself has lost its persuasiveness and we no longer believe in it? In particular, if morality depends on God and we no longer believe in God as a moral force, then might we have lost our faith in the moral world order without yet admit-ting it to ourselves? Why the insistence on reason, he asks, if not that we fear our more "natural" passions and aspirations, as if we need formal principles to keep our spirits in check? And why, he asks, this emphasis on universal prin-ciples, if not in order to impose the same set of bland demands and expectations on everyone, thus stunting the growth of those few who could excel far beyond the others? Morality, Nietzsche concludes, is not justifiable, not because phi-losophers haven't come up with a wholly acceptable justification, but because there is something seriously wrong with the very idea of "morality."

A similar strategy is pursued by the French existentialist, Jean-Paul Sartre. He rejects the attempt to justify morality on the ground that any such justifi-cation will serve only to shift the ultimate responsibility for what we do away from our own free choice. Suppose a young man has to choose between joining the army to fight for his country or staying home with his grieving mother (who has already lost her husband and two sons in the war)? What is the "principle" he should follow in making his decision? And how will this principle justify the decision once he has made it? The fact is that he has to *make* a decision. In doing so, he might endorse a number of principles (such as that one's primary obligation is to one's mother), but both the decision and its justification are nothing other than his having made his choice and having to live with it. The problem is not that of justifying morality, Sartre insists; it is, rather, choosing to live and living in "good faith," which means, among other things, not appealing to any authority, including reason, to support one's own free choices.

The rejection of the whole program of justifying morality has had its most radical and influential successes not in the flamboyant and passionate statements of Nietzsche and the existentialists, however, but in the sober academic pronouncements of English and American analytic philosophers of this century. The most prominent figure in this development was the Cambridge philosopher G. E. Moore, whose "Open Question Argument" we met in the earlier section "Facts and Values." The consequence of that argument was that value claims cannot be proven by any number of facts; one can always ask the "open question"—"Yes, but is it good?" Moore's own response to this conclusion was that "good" is the name of a "simple, undefinable, non-natural property" which we know by "intuition" (thus giving rise to a theory, called "intuitionism," that one knows that something is good by "seeing that it is so," but without being able to prove it). Moore argued that one cannot justify morality in the usual sense (that is, one cannot prove it by appeal to reason or purposes or consequences) but, nevertheless, one can know what is good. On that basis, Moore defended a version of utilitarianism. What he rejected was the traditional "proof" of utilitarianism—exemplified by Mill—in which "good" is identified with a "natural property" such as pleasure.

Moore's followers were not so optimistic about their ability to "intuit" the good; they accepted his "open question argument" but rejected his intuitionism and utilitarianism. They concluded simply that morality and ethics in general, as well as religion, aesthetics and any number of other nonscientific disciplines, are devoid of substantial cognitive content. Attempting to justify them makes no more sense than trying to justify your preference for chocolate fudge ice cream. The leading movement in this wholesale rejection of not only the attempt to justify morality but also of ethics as such was *logical positivism,* a movement which had its origin among a number of German and Austrian philosophers and scientists who were fighting the Nazis in the 1930s. Their view of ethics was that opinions about values are mainly matters of emotion, not knowledge; the ethical theory developed by some of the logical positivists— notably by A. J. Ayer in England and C. L. Stevenson in the United States— was accordingly called *emotivism.* They argued (often following Hume's argument) that value judgments cannot be based wholly on facts and that statements in ethics, therefore, are not matters of knowledge and cannot be justified as matters of fact can be. Thus, the general position of a great many contemporary philosophers has come to be called *noncognitivism,* which means that ethical statements are neither true nor false and cannot be justified as such.

Noncognitivism has had many variants in England and the United States in the past fifty years. Emotivism—the very strong noncognitivist view that making a moral judgment is logically on a par with yelling "Hooray" (A. J. Ayer's formulation)—was popular for a decade or so, but it ran up against a powerful objection, Namely, it left no room at all for an account of *moral reasoning,* that is, an account of how we deliberate and persuade ourselves and others of the rightness or wrongness of an action. Accordingly, noncognitivism moved on to other variants, including a theory of *prescriptivism,* which is still defended today by R. M. Hare of Oxford. This theory accepts the importance of moral reasoning but nevertheless rejects the idea that morality can be justified as such. We can "prescribe" certain forms of behavior to one another (as a physician "prescribes" a medicine), but we cannot prove that they are the *right* forms of behavior.

The obvious problem facing the prescriptivist is the *fanatic,* the person who holds perverted ideas about what is right and wrong and will not listen to our reasoning at all. If a man wants to be respected and trusted by his peers, we can convince him to accept our prescription, "Act such that you will be trusted and respected." But if we are giving prescriptions to a person whom Aristotle calls "the wicked man," Adolf Hitler, for example, our arguments may be utterly ineffective. In such cases, it is hard to swallow the conclusion that we cannot simply say—and *know*—that we are right and the other person is *wrong.* Nevertheless, the prescriptivist theory, like noncognitive theories in general, strikes a sympathetic chord in most twentieth-century readers. It is a point of widespread agreement that ethics is not like science and cannot be "proven," and that, though agreement may be necessary if we are to live together in society, ethics is largely a matter of attitude and consensus, not knowledge.

Undergraduates often sum up this popular position by saying that "value judgments are subjective" and dismiss moral claims with "that's just a value judgment." But the difference between the noncognitivist and the undergraduate subjectivist positions is worth noting: The logical positivists and other noncognitivists developed elaborate theories of language and knowledge in support of their claim that ethics is not a matter of knowledge. The undergraduate subjectivist, however, all too often uses only the glib conclusion and dispenses with the arguments and theories. The logical positivists defended their noncognitivism in order to root out much nonsense from the realm of moral discussion; too many undergraduate subjectivists adopt the noncognitivist position just in order to ward off criticism and to not have to think about ethics at all. But, as many noncognitivists are now arguing, ethical claims nevertheless have their *reasons,* and ethics, even if "subjective," nevertheless requires some objectively valid reasoning.

THE JUSTIFICATION OF MORALITY
AND THE PROBLEM OF RELATIVISM

Why are philosophers so concerned with the justification of morality? In part, they are concerned to know that what we do is right, and that we are justified in encouraging or forcing others (our children, immigrants, and deviants) to conform to our ways. With most social customs, we may be content merely to insist that "that's the way we do things here." We are perfectly willing to accept that people elsewhere—perhaps even our own children—do things differently. But where morality is concerned, as in such issues as sexual behavior and the treatment of children, we are not willing simply to accept these differences. The justification of morality is thus an attack on what we earlier called "relativism"—the view that different people have different moral systems and that no position is more correct than any other. Thus, Kant asserts that morality consists of absolute, unconditional, "categorical" principles, and the utilitarians insist that there is, in fact, a universal standard by which all moralities may be judged, namely, the extent to which they do, or do not, make people happy. The Judeo-Christian tradition takes care of the problem of relativism with the doctrine of one God Who has a single set of moral laws for every people. (Aristotle, it is worth noting, simply assumed that the values of Athenian aristocrats were superior to all others and saw no need to prove the point.)

It is time that we took a closer look at ethical relativism. Is it a plausible thesis? If we were to accept relativism, would ethics, and morality in particular, be undermined? It is often assumed that it would—for example, by the undergraduate subjectivist who insists that "it's all relative." It is also assumed that it would by a great many very sophisticated moral philosophers, who therefore take great pains to dismiss relativism as the nemesis of ethics. They argue, for example, that although the superficial aspects of morals may differ from society to society, the "deep" structures of morals—for example, some version of "the right to life" or some version of "the pursuit of happiness"—are the same the world over. Or, they argue that ethical relativism is, on the face of it, an absurd or self-refuting thesis for one of two reasons: Either the sentence "This is morally good in society X but not in society Y" is meaningless, or the ethical relativist who asserts, as a universal principle, that "different things are considered good in different societies and therefore we *ought* to respect these differences" is stating a contradiction, asserting as a universally correct principle that there are no universally correct principles.

First of all, it is necessary to point out that there are at least two forms of relativism that often become confused in such discussions. There is ethical relativism, which concerns us here, and there is cultural relativism, on which ethical relativism is loosely based. Cultural relativism is a *descriptive* thesis, based on anthropological observation: different cultures do indeed have different ideas about what is right and wrong. Ethical relativism, on the other hand, is the view that what is *right* is relative to different cultures. The denial that there are any "deep" differences in moral matters among cultures is part of the cultural relativity debate. But, on the basis of anthropological observation of the past several centuries, it must be said that this denial is almost certainly false (though this demonstration is in the domain of social science, not in that of ethics). Let us simply assume here that deep moral differences among cultures are an established fact. Not only do people get married in different ways and under different conditions; the very concepts of marriage and family are decidedly different in different cultures. Not only does what counts as stealing vary from culture to culture; the very notion of stealing is absent from some, extremely important in others. But, if these differences are true, does cultural relativism entail ethical relativism?

The answer, immediately, is no. One might well accept differences in various peoples' ideas of right and wrong and yet insist, as Kant did, that some of those ideas are just plain *wrong*. There is no paradox or self-contradiction here. One can accept the fact of diversity in morals without giving an inch to the thesis that one ought to have humility toward one's own moral prejudices and respect for others' values. Cultural relativism does not entail ethical relativism. Indeed, the visibility of the former may only reinforce a moralist's disdain for the latter.

Ethical relativism is itself an ethical thesis. It insists that we not only recognize moral differences but respect them too. Does this view embody a contradiction? If one asserts as a universal principle that everyone everywhere *ought* to respect ethical differences, one is indeed in an awkward position. It is an obvious fact that not everyone agrees with that particular principle. How, then, should the ethical relativist deal with those who disagree? It doesn't make much sense only to say, in line with the relativist thesis, "Oh, well, we simply disagree about that, but you're just as right as I am and I respect your opinion." On the other hand, it is no less paradoxical and absurd for the ethical relativist adamantly to insist that the opponent is wrong. According to whom? According to the relativist's relative standards? Certainly not according to the opponent's own standards.

The problem for the relativist is where to stand while pronouncing the doctrine that one moral view is as correct or incorrect as another. Is he or she living inside a particular culture, in which case the doctrine is certainly false? It may well be that killing one's grandparents by leaving them out on the ice is morally permissible and explicable in certain Eskimo cultures. But though one might be tolerant and argue that grandparricide is right in certain cultures in certain circumstances, this admission is not yet, in any sense, to weaken one's own belief that it is wrong to kill one's grandparents. Stepping outside one's culture (assuming that such a notion is even intelligible for most people) may allow us to say something like, "That's considered moral by them but not by Americans," but this is in no way to suggest that "one morality is as good as another." We have already stepped out of the moral context in which such comparisons are possible.

To accept cultural relativism and to be an ethical relativist does not mean that one cannot compare moral systems, evaluate them, and choose between them. In many cases, two systems will already include principles in common which can therefore be employed to judge one course of action morally better than another. If we disagree with the Australians about their treatment of aborigines, it is not a matter of ethical relativism. They have the same principles of equality and fairness that we do; the dispute is one of politics rather than ethics. If some ultimate good or purpose is shared by two cultures, that good or purpose may also be used to judge one moral system as better or worse. For example, if it is agreed by a communist culture and a capitalist culture (assuming that these are moral as well as economic systems) that the ultimate purpose of each culture is to make its citizens happy and materially comfortable, then there is no question of ethical relativism, but just the straightforward question about which system makes people happier and more comfortable.

The real problem begins when both ultimate principles and purposes clash. We need not go to the islands and jungles explored by anthropologists to see such a problem in progress, however. Consider the abortion issue in the United States. Even without bringing in the religious dimension of the dispute, it is clear that the ultimate principles, "right to life" and "individual freedom," are in direct confrontation (even if both parties accept both principles and disagree only on their priority). But this vehement dispute should show us quite clearly which versions of ethical relativism make sense and which do not. It is easy to see how a person not too involved in the argument can listen to both sides and conclude that "they both have a point." The listener may even get involved and try to choose sides, perhaps without success. But what the observer cannot say, except ironically, is that they are both right and both wrong. Nor is it valid to conclude, because both sides are supported by powerful principles and strong arguments, that "one morality is as correct as another." The conclusion is, rather, that it is possible to have very intense and difficult disagreements in ethics, but only because it is possible to build more than one very persuasive case. It does not follow that it is impossible to build a weak one or have no case at all. Moreover, one of the disputants in the abortion argument might well respect the opinions of the other; indeed, this is more often the case than the most publicized debates would suggest. But respect for one's opponent is not the same as accepting the opponent's view, nor does such respect in any way entail either giving up or weakening one's own view. Indeed, to hold a moral view is, in an important sense, to be unable to consider objectively the alternatives. One might nonetheless be an ethical relativist and firmly believe that one ought to respect the moral views of others. "Respect" is not the same as "agreement," though the naive relativist and the vehement critic of relativism too easily confuse the two.

What about the case in which the principle of mutual tolerance itself is in question, that is, the issue of ethical relativism is itself the subject of ethical dispute? It is here that the ethical relativists find themselves in an impossible dilemma, and the conclusion does indeed seem to be that a relativist cannot consistently and coherently defend that position against someone who insists that morals are not relative (that is, that despite the diversity of moral opinions in the world, there is, nevertheless, a correct moral view—one's own, of course). But it does not follow, as many moralists have too quickly concluded, that ethical relativism itself is an incoherent position. It is not a coherent position applied to itself, but then, this is a common form of paradox throughout the logic of self-reference, and, more important, there is a lot more to ethics and morality than the position of ethical relativism itself.

At its best, ethical relativism may not be that at all but, rather, a moral view in which the principle of tolerance is itself the most important moral principle, at least where other cultures or communities are concerned. On the other hand, ethical relativism may be an excuse for not taking any moral position seriously, including one's own. It is evident that the person who insists on the absolute correctness of his or her own moral position often ignores the other person and displays unwarranted disrespect for not only the other person's views but for the other person as well. The relativist, too, is easily tempted to abuse the ethical relativist position, however. Ethical relativism is not just an abstract thesis; it is also, according to philosopher John Ladd, a strategy, a way of defusing ethical views. By answering a moral claim with the reply, "That's just your opinion," one robs it of its moral force and shifts attention from the moral claim itself to the person making the claim. In other words, it is a technique for dodging the moral issue. Relativism, in its indirect way, may be just as dogmatic and intolerant as moral absolutism, even while attacking dogmatism and intolerance.

If the ethical relativist cannot consistently and coherently defend ethical relativism, does that not mean that the position itself must be wrong? On the other hand, if we can't even make sense of the relativists' position, what sense are we to make of the diversity of moral views in the world? Surely we need some ethical position on the matter. Should we respect the differences and leave others alone (assuming that they don't interfere with us)? Or are we right to impose our morals on the world (even if, however unlikely it seems, our morals may turn out to be wrong)? And, less practically urgent but of ultimate ethical importance: Is our morality ultimately justifiable? Ethicists often suggest that if relativism were true, then ethics would be impossible. At most, we could (like anthropologists) describe our morals, and we could continue to prescribe them, at least to one another. But we could not justify them. Our ethics would be without a foundation, and our prescriptions would be without an ultimate anchor.

This fear, however, is unjustified. To think that the whole of morality turns on the question of justification and the threat of relativism is to turn ethics upside down. The process of justification may succeed from the top down, from the most abstract principles and purposes to the most particular moral judgments. But it does not follow, as many ethicists seem to believe, that the validity of the particular judgments depends upon their support from the more abstract principles discussed above. Whatever the strategy of moral justification, our moral lives proceed from the bottom up—from the ethos in which we were raised and in which most of us continue to live the whole of our lives. Indeed, it may be that we will never agree on even the formulation of the most abstract principles and purposes of morality, much less on their mode of justification. Nevertheless, within our culture, and apart from the exceptional clashes of morals, we do and will continue to agree on most of our day-to-day moral decisions and judgments. Ethics does not depend on the success of philosophers' finding an adequate justification for morality as a whole. The emphasis on justification may itself be an essential part of our ethics, but it does not follow that the only adequate justification must be an absolute and singular foundation for the whole of morality. It is the nature of justification that it always reaches further, for broader and better reasons. It is not always possible to find such reasons, but our morality is not endangered. As long as we are within our ethos, our ethics remains intact. Outside of any ethos, there may be no answer to the quest for ultimate justification, but neither is it at all obvious that, outside of any ethos, there is anything left to justify.

ETHICS, ETHOS, AND PLURALISM: AMERICAN MORALITY TODAY

Once upon a time, we like to imagine, when morality was a simple matter and when everyone agreed on what was right and what was wrong, the questions of justification and ethical relativism could not have even been conceived of, much less pursued seriously. It is unlikely, however, that there has ever been such a time. The world is a small place, and cultures are forever colliding, throwing moralities as well as national interests and religions into conflict with one another. Aristotle tried to present a picture of Athenian morality that was a unified, generally agreed-upon whole, with no need for justification and not even a bow to alternative moralities. The image, however, is misleading, as even a cursory look at the history of his period will show. Aristotle's Greece was already a cauldron of conflicts of culture, both within Greek society and between Greeks and the "barbarians" around them. In our culture, the melting pot for most of the cultures of the world, cultural conflicts are the rule of life, for which we try to compensate by inventing a single bland name which will encompass them all. We use the term "pluralism," as if it were itself a single ethic rather than a constant battle for ethnic survival, ethical recognition, and moral superiority.

It is in recognition of the plurality of mores and morals by which we live that theories of ethics, especially in the United States, have tended toward non-cognitivism. By denying that ethics is a matter of truth and falsehood, by denying that one can justify a single correct moral position, the noncognitivist makes room for the plurality of opinions that constitute the complex ethos of contemporary American society. Accordingly, it is important to understand such views, not just as metaethical theories about the justification of morality, but also as expressions of a particular ethical point of view. What would that be?

In his recent book *After Virtue,* Alasdair MacIntyre has analyzed emotivism and other noncognitive theories of morality as the expression of a culture which has all but lost sight of morality and its essential nature. It is as though some grave catastrophe had destroyed our whole language and practice of morality, MacIntyre suggests, and all that is left are a few scattered words (like "ought" and "moral") and a debatable collection of principles whose point and purpose have been forgotten. Emotivism and other noncognitive theories, he then hypothesizes, are not so much metaethical theories about the nature of ethics and its language as they are the philosophical expressions of a culture in which moral claims actually have lost their purpose, in which it is generally accepted that we will never agree on such basic ethical issues as the right to life of unborn fetuses, the justifiability of war, and the justice of taxation and the redistribution of wealth. But if we compare this ethical confusion with the ethos which we at least seem to find in Aristotle and the Greeks, for example, the difference is shocking; Aristotle regularly appeals to such general agreement among his fellow citizens, and the idea that ethical issues might be undecidable and a matter of "mere personal opinion" would have struck him and his fellows as the most dangerous kind of utter nonsense.

What is missing in our ethics, in other words, is a sense of an ethos, an already established and agreed-upon way of living in which values are shared and unquestioned and in which the question of ultimate justification is not essential but is only of secondary importance. Given an ethos, this does not mean that one cannot justify and criticize principles and actions within the ethos. Quite the contrary, the established values and principles in the ethos provide the secure basis for justifying and criticizing particular rules and actions. What one cannot do is to try to stand outside one's ethos and evaluate or justify *all* its values and principles. To do so is to leave oneself without any basis whatsoever for making the evaluation and so without any foundation for justifying the basic principles, that is, the morality, of that ethos. Desires and purposes must be accepted at face value within the ethos. (What would it be like to play soccer but reject the idea that one ought to kick the ball into the goal?) They are an "open question" outside of it. (Apart from any game, what would it mean to insist that one ought to kick a ball between two posts?) The dictates and principles of reason will be "self-evident" within the ethos but arbitrary and unprovable without it. The various sentiments and emotional reactions a person has within the ethos will quite naturally be the cultivated products of one's upbringing with that ethos, but outside of any ethos, all sentiments and emotional reactions will seem merely accidental and provincial. Without an ethos, in other words, there is no basis for the justification of morality. Within an ethos, however, no ultimate justification is possible or necessary. Indeed, such an exercise may even seem utterly without purpose.

MacIntyre thus analyzes not just a recent movement in ethics but our entire culture as the disintegration of the communal and cultural contexts within which morality and the virtues alone make sense. The quest for justification he traces back to the Enlightenment of the eighteenth century, when the European sense of ethos was already falling apart and the search for universal values and principles was taken up in earnest by way of compensation. We have already noted that Plato and Aristotle did not engage in the quest for justification that is central to modern ethics. (Insofar as they did so, Nietzsche argues, it was because their Greek society too was already past its "Golden Age" and starting to decay.) David Hume's rejection of the justification of morality was just part and parcel of the skeptical ethical atmosphere within which the quest for justification was being carried out, accordingly, and Nietzsche, in MacIntyre's analysis, was simply the final, fatal blow to an already collapsing system of morality (an image that Nietzsche adopted for himself).

What MacIntyre suggests might too easily be mistaken for nostalgic despair and an impossible plea to return to a mythical past. ("Forward to the twelfth century," he half-jokingly comments.) But his point is not just a negative one (indeed, this is precisely his criticism of the whole ethical tradition from Hume to Moore and the noncognitivists). It is rather a warning about both our current attitudes toward ethics and the philosophical theories in which they are expressed. We make too much of an ideal out of being "above" any particular society and culture and so, in the name of universalism, find ourselves nowhere at all. We insist on rationally justifying our moral principles and end up wondering on what grounds we could condemn even a Hitler or a sadist. ("If there is no justification, everything is permitted.") But to have an ethics is not to have a rigid set of moral principles with an ironclad theory of justification for them; it is to be part of an ethos in which morality plays an accepted and unquestioned role, and justification is unnecessary. To question everything is to be left with nothing, and the failure to find an ultimate justification then seems to undermine morality itself. But what is worse are the conclusions often drawn from this. Namely, either:

1 We're hopelessly confused, swimming in a veritable sea of values without any hope of common agreement (and so all values are "just a matter of personal opinion")

or

2 Our group is right and everyone else is wrong (or worse—sinful, perverted, or damned).

Either way, ethics is unpleasant and the good life is an uncomfortable compromise, at best.

What we need, therefore, is a new ethics of pluralism, an ethics especially suited to contemporary America, rather than the ancient Greek polis or the small-town German morality described by Kant as the universal moral law. The naive and lazy relativist view that "values are just a matter of personal opinion" must be recognized as just as nonsensical and dangerous as the dogmatic view that one's own morals are absolutely correct and everyone else is wrong or worse. We are not a society without values, much less a society in which every act is no better and no worse than any other. But we are a society with a multiplicity of values, in which it therefore becomes all the more urgent for each of us to clarify, understand, and, within modest limits, justify our values and our views. The *ethē* of most traditional societies are already established, but the complex ethos that constitutes American society is still in the making. It is by doing ethics that we help in its formation.

INDEX